"NO SINGLE IN
ON OPEN-AIR PREACHING AND EVANGELISM IN THE
LAST CENTURY THAN RAY COMFORT."

Jesus did it. Paul did it. Old Testament prophets did it, and you *should* do it. Thanks to Ray's new book, you *can* do it.

Ray Comfort is on the Mount Rushmore of Open-Air Preachers. No single individual has had more impact on open-air preaching and evangelism in the last century than Ray Comfort. Why would we not want to learn from a modern-day giant?

His hard-earned wisdom will equip you with everything you need to know about sharing the gospel in the open air. When it comes to open-air preaching, no one has more road miles than Ray Comfort. Glean from his wisdom, and hit the streets.

—TODD FRIEL, *host of Wretched TV and Radio*

Some people say that street evangelism is more of a deterrent in today's postmodern culture and that it's more about relational evangelism. You really can't make a statement like that. Look at some of the things God called His prophets to do: go stand in the street, go preach, do this. You can't say that street preaching is bad today or it was good in Whitefield's time. It's always been a scandal.

There are people who are gifted at street preaching and I really appreciate them. One of them is my friend Ray Comfort. He is just gifted at street preaching because he can stand there and tell you things and you may get as mad as a hornet but you still see the love that he has and the kindness and everything. All witnessing is relational; all preaching is relational. It is; it's just a different way. Ray Comfort can have forty people around him and be preaching on the street and be relational to all of them.

It is obvious that Ray loves God and has been called to proclaim the gospel to the lost. I have watched him be cruelly caricatured, mocked, threatened, cursed, and spit upon. And yet, his love for the unconverted remains undaunted and his boldness untempered. He seems to personify Psalm 126:6, "He who goes to and fro weeping, carrying his bag of seed, shall indeed come again with a shout of joy, bringing his sheaves with him" (NASB). I praise God for this grace that has been given to Brother Comfort and am encouraged to carry on in my own station by his example. May he remain faithful to the end.

—**PAUL DAVID WASHER**, *Founder/Director,*
HeartCry Missionary Society

FIFTY YEARS
OF OPEN-AIR
PREACHING
EVERYTHING I'VE LEARNED

RAY COMFORT

BRIDGE
LOGOS

Newberry, FL 32669

Fifty Years of Open-Air Preaching: Everything I've Learned

Published by:
Bridge-Logos
Newberry, Florida 32669, USA
bridgelogos.com

Printed in the United States of America

ISBN 978-1-61036-906-0

Library of Congress Control Number: 2024938229

Edited by Lynn Copeland

Cover photo by Carri Roman

Page design and layout by Genesis Group (genesis-group.net)

Originally published as *The Word on the Street: How to Share the Gospel in the Open-Air* (ISBN 978-1-61036-247-4)

Open-air preaching:
Going somewhere I don't want to go
to preach a message I don't want to preach
to people who don't want to hear it.
But the love of Christ compels me.

Dedicated to Stuart Scott,
a faithful servant

CONTENTS

INTRODUCTION

Our Lord himself, who is yet more our pattern,
delivered the larger proportion of his sermons on
the mountain's side, or by the seashore, or in the
streets. Our Lord was to all intents and purposes
an open-air preacher.

—CHARLES SPURGEON

hank you for picking up this book. Whether you are experienced in sharing the gospel with individuals and now want to reach more people through preaching in the open air, or you're just getting started with evangelizing and want to dive into the deep end with open-air preaching as I did, your voice is greatly needed. To many, the practice of preaching to strangers seems archaic and outdated, and we rarely hear pastors preaching on the subject despite its mention throughout Scripture. Perhaps that's because they don't practice it themselves. Let's hope and pray that changes. Your example may help, so God bless you for your boldness.

Some have wondered whether open-air preaching is for every Christian. I would say yes and no. Yes, if you desperately want to reach the world with the gospel. No, if you are not that desperate. Mark 16:15 is commonly called "the Great Commission," and it tells us to "go into all the world and preach the gospel to every creature." The word "preach" means to "herald" with a raised voice. Open-air preaching is as old as preaching itself. Throughout history God has used open-air preachers to bring the gospel to the multitudes. Not only did Jesus preach the gospel in the open air, but so did John the Baptist, Paul, Stephen, Peter, John Wesley, George Whitefield, Charles Spurgeon, D. L. Moody, and many others throughout church history.

In fact, Charles Spurgeon, known as the Prince of Preachers, said, "No sort of defense is needed for preaching out-of-doors; but it would need very potent arguments to prove that a man had done his duty who has never preached beyond the walls of his meetinghouse." John Wesley stated, "What marvel the devil does not love field-preaching! Neither do I: I love a commodious room, a soft cushion, a handsome pulpit. But where is my zeal if I do not trample all these underfoot to save one more soul?"

> *"We are not to preach merely to those who come to listen. We must carry the Gospel to where men do not desire it. We should consider it our business to be generously impertinent—thrusting the Gospel into men's way—whether they will hear or whether they will not."* —CHARLES SPURGEON

When I witness one-to-one, I am excited that one person is listening to the words of everlasting life. In a good open air, I can witness one-to-two hundred. How much better it is to offer the cure to death and Hell to two hundred than one dying sinner. Whitefield spoke in the open air to crowds of up to twenty thousand! I wish every Christian could say with the apostles, "We cannot but speak the things which we have seen and heard"

(Acts 4:20), to a point where they would open-air preach to those unaware that they are on their way to Hell.

Perhaps the thought of open-air preaching is new to you. You can't picture yourself standing up among strangers and preaching the gospel to them. But if we are serious about reaching this world, let us emulate Jesus and the apostles and preach where sinners gather. *In thirty minutes, a good open-air preacher can reach more unsaved people than the average church does in a year.* Thank God the disciples didn't stay in the upper room. They didn't carpet the building, pad the pews, then put a notice on the front door stating "Tonight: Gospel outreach service, 7 p.m. All welcome." They went out and preached in the open air.

The gospel is for the world, not the church. That's why Jesus said, "Go...," but like King Og, we seem to have it backwards. We take sinners to meetings rather than meetings to sinners. The church prefers to fish on dry land rather than get its feet wet. But there is no higher calling than to follow in the footsteps of the Savior and preach in the open air.

ARE YOU QUALIFIED?

Perhaps you lack the courage to do such a thing. Congratulations; you have just qualified yourself for the job. If you consider yourself a "nobody" with nothing to offer God, you are His material. When you submit yourself to Him for His use, He promises to do "exceedingly abundantly above all that we ask or think, according to the power that works in us" (Ephesians 3:20). God in His wisdom has chosen the weak things of the world to put to shame the mighty and the foolishness of preaching to save those who believe.

Now all you need is a compassion that will swallow your fear, and a conscience that will give you no rest until you break the sound barrier. I pray that, through this book, God will give you both.

You will notice numerous links throughout this book to videos that you can watch online. This is because we tend to remember what we see more than what we simply read. It is far more instructive and encouraging to actually see and hear open-air preaching than to just read about it. You will see the power of God's Law to stop the sinner's mouth, how a heckler can be used to draw a crowd, and many other principles that will help you not only to grow in Christ but to conquer your fears.

CHAPTER 1

A LITTLE PERSONAL HISTORY

*I believe I never was more acceptable to my
Master than when I was standing to teach those
hearers in the open fields... I now preach to ten
times more people than I would if I had been
confined to the churches.*

—GEORGE WHITEFIELD

The year was 1974. I was riding the bus to my shop, Leather-gear, where I manufactured dressy made-to-order leather and suede jackets. The store was about half a mile from the center of my home city of Christchurch, New Zealand, which was built around an Anglican cathedral in The Square.

For two years, I had rented a building close to our home in the suburbs, six miles from The Square. It was a combined leather gear and surf shop. One day a stranger boldly walked into the store saying that he had purchased the property and wanted me out in a month. It was ironic because I had been a

Christian for a month or so and had just given my business to the Lord. I wanted everything to be in His hands.

A month later, I was joyfully making jackets from home rent-free, but it wasn't long before the city said I couldn't use a commercial sewing machine in a residential area. Very strangely, I couldn't find anywhere near our home where I could set up a business. Every door I knocked on closed in my face. I was forced to find a building closer to the heart of the city of 350,000 souls.

As I sat on the bus heading into town, I looked at those who were seated around me. I had found everlasting life, and I knew that if these people died in their sins, they would go to Hell. But it wasn't just that terrible fact that bothered me. I was aware that each of them was tormented by the dread of death, something I had before I was saved (see Hebrews 2:14,15). It was an overwhelming feeling of hopeless horror—that this thing called "death" was waiting to swallow me.

> *"God forbid that I should travel with anybody a quarter of an hour without speaking of Christ to them."*
> —GEORGE WHITEFIELD

Oh, how utterly thankful I was that God had saved me from death: "For You have delivered my soul from death, my eyes from tears, and my feet from falling" (Psalm 116:8). Words can't begin to express the gratitude I had for the hope of the gospel; and these poor souls, as far as I knew, were unsaved . . . waiting to die. The thought horrified me. If I stood up and preached to them, the bus would stop and I would be tossed out; so I whispered, "If only there was some place I could preach to people. If only . . ."

Two weeks later (through a series of strange circumstances), the city legalized public speaking in The Square. Oh, dear. It seemed that God had answered my prayer.

MY FIRST OPEN AIR

So it was that I found myself standing in front of a small crowd in The Square, waiting to preach the gospel to thirty to forty people sitting on the steps eating lunch, with a few stragglers leaning against a wall. To say I was nervous would be the understatement of eternity. Seven years earlier, I had determined never, ever to speak in public. Ever. My high school teacher had required the class to give speeches, and I had dried up in the middle of my speech about surfing, had to sit down, and was humiliated in front of my friends. Yet here I was, about to open my terrified mouth in front of strangers who weren't going to like what I was about to say.

I felt very nervous, but I knew I had to do it. Just as I was about to step forward, a Christian came alongside me not knowing what I was planning to do. I can't remember his exact words, but it was something like, "Look at that bunch of losers. Hardly worth preaching the gospel to them," then he walked off. I couldn't believe my ears. It was perfect timing. Too perfect. I realized it was a subtle satanic message to discourage me, so I stepped forward and preached anyway. I have no memory of how I began or even how the crowd reacted, but after I finished I knew it wasn't over. I knew I had to come back and do it again and again.

That was around March 1974, and I thank God that I opened my mouth that day. It was the first of over three thousand times that I would speak to the crowds in "Speaker's Corner" in The Square.

I certainly wasn't the only speaker who took advantage of the audience gathered there. Over the fourteen years in which I preached in Christchurch, I befriended a colorful character known as "the Wizard," who also regularly spoke to the lunchtime crowds. He was intelligent, friendly, kind, and very anti-Christian. However, he liked me despite the fact that I was a "disgusting, low-down, born-again," while he was a High-Church Anglican. I preached for the first lunch hour and he preached for the second.

This is a typical crowd that would gather to listen to the Wizard (my friendly enemy). At times he would kindly allow me to climb his ladder and preach to his huge crowds.

His crowds were always larger than mine, but because of our friendship, there were times when he let me climb up on his ladder and speak to his crowd while he stood beside me. It was amazing.

Here is Jack (the Wizard) in his John the Baptist outfit. He would, with tongue-in-check, ask his crowd who looked more like Jesus, him or me?

On January 10, 1989, Sue and I left our beloved city and families and left everything we knew to be home. I had been invited to take my family to the United States, specifically to bring a teaching called "Hell's Best Kept Secret" to the church of America. For a video clip of the Wizard on the day I left New Zealand, go to LivingWaters.com/OAP and watch "Speaker's Corner 1989."

CHANGING VENUES

Following our move to Los Angeles, I made sure that I continued open-air preaching. For a year I traveled to the famed MacArthur Park and preached to addicts.

Before we arrived in the United States, I was absolutely sure that God wanted me to go to MacArthur Park. I had no idea that it had the dubious reputation of having the highest crime rate in the Los Angeles area. I remember preaching with my back to a tree because someone warned me that if I didn't, I would probably be stabbed. I didn't doubt it. The place was a haven for drug abuse.

I ended up not only preaching, but feeding the hungry and bathing wounds. The people were so hungry they would fight over the sandwiches I gave out and I had to warn them not to rush at me to get food. One time I had them line up and instructed them to take just one sandwich each. I couldn't believe my eyes when, just after telling them to take only one, I could see a man with a sandwich in one hand reaching out for another! I was indignant and said, "What's that in your hand?!" He said, "A knife," to which I replied, "Here, have another sandwich." It was a very memorable place.[1]

After preaching weekly at MacArthur Park for a year, there was a big police bust and my "congregation" ended up either in prison or scattered throughout Los Angeles. I went on a search for them and ended up on Fourth Street in downtown Los Angeles, where the homeless slept on the sidewalk by the hundreds if not thousands. I would take a team to preach the gospel and then give out food. We did that many times until the Los Angeles riots occurred in the area where I took my team and I decided it was too dangerous to continue going there.

That's when I started taking a team to the Third Street Promenade in Santa Monica, a popular shopping and dining area filled with endless tourists and colorful characters.

One Friday night Arnold Schwarzenegger and his wife walked past. I decided that wise men follow stars, so I followed him and noticed that they walked into one of the well-known Gap stores.

"The great benefit of open-air preaching is that we get so many newcomers to hear the gospel who otherwise would never hear it." —CHARLES SPURGEON

I entered through another door and waited for them to approach me. So there I was, standing in the gap for Arnold Schwarzenegger. As he approached I became starstruck and didn't greet them but instead just held out a tract. He put out his hand and said a loud, "No!" and walked on. I was annoyed with myself for not at least having the courtesy of telling him how great his movies were (even though I had never seen one) before offering him a tract. Fortunately, a few minutes later a young member of my team got to witness to him and his wife for about ten minutes. The next week, three times as many church members wanted to come with me to Santa Monica.

I preached there every Friday night for three and a half years until being forced to move on by a professing Christian. He would show up with a bull horn and drown me out with abuse. I felt it was time for a change. For a video clip of preaching at Santa Monica during that time, go to LivingWaters.com/OAP and watch "Santa Monica July 2001."

I then began frequenting the local courts in our home city of Bellflower and witnessing one to one with people who were waiting to see the judge. One day I arrived earlier than normal and noticed that fifty to sixty people were lined up outside waiting to get in to the courts. So I made up my mind that I was going to preach to them. I did—and they listened (they were a captive audience).

So almost daily for the next two and a half years, "E.Z." (my son-in-law) and I and a few other members of our staff began open-air preaching at the local courts, to people from all walks of life, then handing out gospel tracts and books to the crowd. One day a judge who didn't like what we were doing, with a stroke of his pen, decreed the area where we stood to preach to be the private property of the court rather than public property. He then made it against the law for us to preach there.

To hear recordings of open-air preaching at the courts, go to LivingWaters.com/springboards and select the audio files.

> *"Oh, to realize that souls, precious, never dying souls, are perishing all around us, going out into the blackness of darkness and despair, eternally lost, and yet to feel no anguish, shed no tears, know no travail! How little we know of the compassion of Jesus!"* —OSWALD J. SMITH

Stuart Scott and I began traveling each Saturday to Huntington Beach and preaching to the crowds there—something we have done weekly since 2006.

Also, during those years, I took teams to prestigious universities around the country (including Yale, USC, UCLA, and Berkeley) and open-air preached to students, shining the light of the gospel in areas darkened by the dogma of evolutionary humanism. We've been commanded to "go into all the world and preach the gospel" (Mark 16:15), so we also went to Europe and preached open air in thirteen European countries in thirteen days and filmed thirteen episodes for our TV program, *Way of the Master*.[2]

Here is part of a crowd at UCLA in 2011.
They stayed for two hours and listened to the gospel.

Over the decades I've been a Christian, I've had the privilege of preaching the gospel in the open air thousands of times, to small handfuls or several hundreds, to young and old, eager listeners and angry crowds, from beaches to university campuses, by myself and with a team, across the country and around the world. I've learned a lot about what to do—and what not to do—to effectively share the gospel in the open air. To save you some of the trial and error, I'd like to share some valuable lessons that I've learned through those experiences. I hope this information will help to shorten your learning curve and help you become even more effective in reaching the lost.

CHAPTER 2

PREPARING YOUR HEART AND MIND

One of the earliest things a minister should do when he leaves college and settles in a country town or village is to begin open-air speaking.

—CHARLES SPURGEON

I t was on a Friday night in the late 1990s, in the famous Third Street Promenade in Santa Monica. I had been open-air preaching to a crowd of thirty to forty people when a very vocal young woman began yelling at me using the F-word. I said, "Madam, can you watch your language? There are ladies present." She said, "I'm a lady," to which I replied, "Madam, you may be a woman, but you're not a lady."

That's when she ran at me like a bat out of heaven and beat me to a pulp. Like a pro, she delivered six punches to my fragile little body. Most females scratch and pull hair, but not this angry woman. She knew how to punch where it hurt. When my team pulled her away from me, she said, "Let me get my purse!"

They made the mistake of letting her go, and that's when she got in a powerful kidney punch. It took two weeks for the bruising to go away. She did, however, double my crowd … and I was able to keep preaching. So she can come back anytime she wants.

Of course, it was my fault that I was beaten up. Experiences like that, and many others over the years, have taught me wonderful lessons that I want to pass on to you, so that you don't make the same mistakes.

DEALING WITH FEARS

The fear we feel when it comes to sharing our faith is very real, even though it's irrational. If we were going to be burned at the stake for being a Christian, or thrown to hungry lions, then our fear would make sense. But it's nevertheless very real and it can paralyze us if we listen to it. So how can we just ignore it?

Imagine you see a four-year-old child fall into an icy swimming pool. I'm sure that you would ignore any thought of the cold water and immediately dive in, because you are thinking of something infinitely more important than your comfort: the life of a human being. That's the mentality you and I must have with evangelism. We need to forget about how our flesh feels and instead think about what awaits people if they die in their sins.

Here is something else to think about. How would you and I describe the character of a person who could stand at the edge of the pool and let the child drown because the water was too cold? Then we need to apply that name to ourselves, if we let fear hinder us from speaking to the lost.

Do you remember how Zacharias, the father of John the Baptist, was struck dumb because he didn't believe God's promise? The angel said to him, "But behold, you will be mute and not able to speak until the day these things take place, because you did not believe my words which will be fulfilled in their own time" (Luke 1:20).

Perhaps you and I can identify with Zacharias. It's our lack of faith in God that causes us to be struck dumb when it comes to sharing our faith. If we fully trusted God, we wouldn't hesitate to open our mouths. If we find ourselves in that position, we should do what Zacharias did when he wanted to say something. He called for a "writing tablet" and used the written word.

> "The open-air speaker's calling is as honorable as it is arduous, as useful as it is laborious. God alone can sustain you in it, but with Him at your side you will have nothing to fear."
> —CHARLES SPURGEON

If you and I are too timid to witness or preach, then we should use the written word by giving out gospel tracts. It's better to do that than do nothing. But then let that give you the confidence to speak to one person, then perhaps to a few gathered around you,... and eventually to a crowd in an open-air setting.

ENTERING THE BATTLE

Experts tell us that most deaths from skydiving happen because of "human error," insinuating that careful skydivers will be okay. In reality, one jumper in every 100,000 fall to their deaths. Instead, if you are bored with life and want an adrenaline rush, try open-air preaching. It's more dangerous than skydiving (see Acts 7:57–60), arguably more scary, and infinitely more productive. And if your life is taken from you while you are preaching, at least your death will not be from human error. Rather, it will be by divine permission.

I have a friend who works for the US Customs Department. He's about 6'3", has a deep voice, and looks like how you'd imagine a federal agent to look. He flies jets that chase drug runners. Tough guy. Yet he said, "I have been skydiving, scuba diving, and drag racing, have ridden motorcycles and flown jets and helicopters, but by far the scariest thing I ever did was to get up on a soapbox and preach the gospel. But as soon as I stepped off that box I couldn't wait to get up and preach again." I know exactly what he meant.

The second day I preached in Christchurch I was more nervous than the first. This is probably because after preaching once I had eased my restless conscience. I could then say to that nagging voice, "I did it, now back off." So the second time I didn't have the provocation of my conscience; it was simply a matter of my will. Would I preach because I cared about people, or was it all about getting rid of guilt? Day after day I had that same feeling that had me visiting the restroom multiple times each morning before I rode my bike the mile or so from my leather shop to The Square. This went on for about three months. Finally, after preaching that many times I was still nervous but it became more under control.

However, even after thousands of times, it remains a matter of discipline. It is a matter of setting my face like flint and ignoring negative thoughts, fears, tiredness, and other things that want to take priority. When I get texts today asking if I will be preaching open air at Huntington Beach, I usually reply, "Is the pope a sinner?" Of course I will be open-air preaching, God willing—and I know He is.

We are soldiers in the most real of wars. No soldier fights on his own whims. I dare to say that few want to enter the heat of battle, but they go because they are not their own. They go because they've been instructed to go. That's the essence of soldiering. So as you enter the battlefield, keep in mind that courage isn't the absence of fear, but the conquering of it.

If we really care for the lost, each of us must learn to push aside the fear of man and replace it with a healthy fear of God. How could we not obey Almighty God when He has commanded us to speak to the lost?

MEDITATE ON GOD

One way to cultivate that most necessary preaching virtue—the fear of God—is to meditate on His works. Most days I'm preoccupied with the mundane, but every now and then I try to move away from normality and push myself into meditative exploration. Or, to put it another way, I stop what I'm doing and think.

My wife, Sue, and I once purchased a pair of Gouldian finches. When I look at the colorful male I wonder what sort of power could create his legs, with their covering of living skin, the tiny nerve-filled bones with ligaments that grew in proportion as the bird grew, with its life-giving blood, its muscles, and its claws that are designed to perfectly grip branches. How did God make its thousands of feathers, each of them fanning out and also growing in proportion as the bird grew, with their different design and angle of entry into the flesh, with their brilliant colors, each growing to a certain size then stopping when it is the right proportion for flight?

How could He create the bird's eyes with automatic lubrication, with their unique upper and lower eyelids that simultaneously and repeatedly blink, with automatic focusing muscles—eyes that see sights and then send instant messaging to an amazingly intricate brain for processing and decision-making?

How did He instill the instinct to gather with others of the same species, and then to seek a mate, build a nest, rear and feed its young? How did God create wings that are made of amazingly light and hollow bones and an intricate system of muscles that could furnish its ability to fly, to balance, and to land on a dime? How did He instill its ability to sing, to look for food and drink, to know what to eat and where to sleep? How did God make its life-sustaining liver, its blood-beating heart, its automatic breath-drawing lungs, and give the bird the necessary confidence to fly?

All the while I'm thinking about this I'm limiting myself to one tiny bird, because my mind can't comprehend that it's just one among millions of birds, among millions of animals, among millions of stars in a massive universe.

Then it dawns on me that I'm using the brain that He created to think about Him and His unspeakable power. Suddenly a fuse goes and my brain blows. I can't handle the overload. And so I pull back from my meditative exploration because it's too much for my tiny mind, and I go back to thinking about eating my next bowl of cereal. Such thoughts when entertained help to cultivate a fear of God, and help us to determine to be true and faithful in our gospel proclamation.

"WATCH IT, BLIND MAN!"

There is one passage in Scripture to which I point for all those who want to evangelize in the open air. It is 2 Timothy 2:24–26:

And a servant of the Lord must not quarrel but be gentle to all, able to teach, patient, in humility correcting those who are in opposition, if God perhaps will grant them repentance, so that they may know the truth, and that they may come to their senses and escape the snare of the devil, having been taken captive by him to do his will. (2 Timothy 2:24–26)

Memorize it. Scripture tells us that sinners are blind. They *cannot* see. What would you think if I were to stomp up to a blind man who had just stumbled, and say, "Watch where you're going, blind man!"? Such an attitude is completely unreasonable. The man *cannot* see.

> "Most Christians would like to send their recruits to Bible College for five years. I would like to send them to hell for five minutes. That would do more than anything else to prepare them for a lifetime of compassionate ministry."
> —WILLIAM BOOTH

The same applies to the lost—spiritual sight is beyond their ability. Look at the words used in Scripture: "whose minds the god of this age has *blinded*" (2 Corinthians 4:4), "the natural man does not receive the things of the Spirit of God, for they are foolishness to him; nor *can* he know them" (1 Corinthians 2:14), "having their understanding *darkened*...because of the *blindness* of their heart" (Ephesians 4:18), "*never able* to come to the knowledge of the truth" (2 Timothy 3:7, emphasis added).

With these thoughts in mind, read 2 Timothy 2:24–26 again and look at the adjectives used by Paul to describe the attitude we are to have with sinners: "must not quarrel...be gentle... patient...in humility." Just as it is unreasonable to be impatient with a blind man, so it is with the sinner.

Among many other things, the Book of Proverbs has taught me the importance of "discretion." The dictionary defines it as "the quality of being careful about what you do and say so that people will not be embarrassed or offended." You will need this virtue if you want to reach your hearers.

Some time ago two teenagers were sitting in their car with the doors open listening to very loud rap music across from our house. They didn't seem to notice that the neighborhood trees were bent over by the loudness of their sound. Next door to the teenage jam session lives a frail elderly couple, and I could imagine their bones rattling as they sat in their chairs, too afraid to say anything because of horror stories of people being shot to death over loud music.

It was my concern for my elderly neighbors that caused me to grab two powerful weapons and confront the teens. One was a dozen fresh eggs from our chickens, and the other was our "Genius" DVD about John Lennon. I walked up to them and asked, "Hey, guys, would you like a dozen fresh eggs?" They enthusiastically took them. Then I gave them the DVD and added, "You wouldn't mind turning the music down a little, would you? It's booming through our house like a row of cannon balls, and I can't imagine what it's doing to the elderly couple next door."

It worked. The music stopped, our house quit shaking, and no one was shot. How true the words "the better part of valor is discretion, in the which better part I have saved my life" (Henry IV, Part One). I guess Shakespeare read Proverbs.

So cultivate the principle of discretion with your neighbors and with your crowd. Be polite, humble, and kind, but never to a point of bowing to the pressure to compromise the gospel. You are going to feel pressured because there are three things in the Bible that the world hates to hear about: sin, righteousness, and judgment. There are three things in the Bible that we must never leave out of our preaching: sin, righteousness, and judgment. So preach without compromising, but make sure love and discretion are the spring of all you do.

I CAN'T SING, AND WHY IT DOESN'T MATTER

I am forever fascinated by good harmony. God has put unseen and rarely-mentioned laws in place so that music will be music to our ears. But when these laws are violated, the so-called music becomes nothing but an irritation. A person who can't sing in tune is often considered to be "tone deaf." The Bible speaks of "skillful" musicians (see 1 Chronicles 25:7), and those who aren't skilled musically should sing on a hill far away. They shouldn't be singing publicly. I consider myself to be in that category.

I not only find it difficult to hold a tune, if someone next to me breaks into harmony, I can't help but follow them—like a lost and confused sheep. It embarrasses me to admit it, but I can hardly clap in time. The fact that I can't sing doesn't really matter. I simply tone it down publicly. The only one who ever hears me sing is my wife. I'm not embarrassed for her to hear me, because I know that she loves me, and love covers a multitude of sings.

However, when it comes to proclaiming the gospel, we must never tone it down—not even if the whole world is offended. If our talk of sin irritates the lost, we must continue to lift up our voice like a trumpet and show this people their transgression (see Isaiah 58:1).

If, however, we can achieve the right tone, there is a way to speak about the difficult issues without undue offense. And that's what we want. While it may be easy to speak about the love of God with a loving tone, it's not so easy to speak about sin and its frightening consequences. I'm talking about talking about Hell. And that's our dilemma.

The world is asleep in their sins; they're not conscious of their moral condition. But they're not merely asleep. They're asleep and their house is on fire! Our responsibility (with the help of God) is to awaken them and hopefully alarm them. We want them to be concerned to a point where they will run out of the house. So what tone should we use to make this happen? It should be one of love mingled with fear:

> And on some have compassion, making a distinction; but others save with fear, pulling them out of the fire, hating even the garment defiled by the flesh. (Jude 22,23)

The lost will never be awakened if our tone isn't shaped by love and directed by a sense of urgency. Consider how an angel of the Lord awakened sleeping Peter:

> And when Herod was about to bring him out, that night Peter was sleeping, bound with two chains between two soldiers; and the guards before the door were keeping the prison. Now behold, an angel of the Lord stood by him, and a light shone in the prison; and he struck Peter on the side and raised him up, saying, "Arise quickly!" (Acts 12:7,8)

Notice that it wasn't the light that awakened him. He wasn't even aware of it until the angel struck him. Like sleeping Peter, the world doesn't see the light of the gospel. They're not even aware of its glorious truth. The gospel doesn't awaken them because that's not its function. Good news doesn't "alarm." Rather, the sleeping world needs to be struck by the Law because its function is to awaken. Paul said, "I would not have known sin except through the law" (Romans 7:7). He wasn't conscious of his state before God (and his consequent danger) until the Law did its work and awakened him.

The key to having the right tone as we speak to dying sinners about these life-and-death issues is to manifest the love of Jesus—"For the love of Christ controls and compels us..." (2 Corinthians 5:14, AMP). It's not something we conjure up. The mouth merely speaks from the abundance of a loving heart.

LET LOVE BE YOUR MOTIVE

You will need to continually check the spirit in which you speak. Be careful of sarcasm, condescension, or a self-righteous spirit. It's easy to react in a sinful manner when people call you names, cuss at you, say things that aren't true, talk over you, and twist your words. The key is to always let love be your motivation. We don't like rejection or humiliation, and it's only the love of God in us that can give us the grace to handle such things.

It is a sad testimony to our lack of love that we had to be *commanded* to "preach the gospel to every creature" (Mark 16:15). It reveals something about our sinful character. When we are held captive to our fears it reveals our lack of love. What would you think of a doctor who had a cure to cancer in his hand, and had to be *commanded* to take it to his dying patients? Imagine if you asked him why he was hesitating and he said, "I'm afraid they will laugh at me" or, "It's not my gifting to take it to them," or, "I don't know what to say to them." As Charles Spurgeon said, "We must be ashamed at the mere suspicion of unconcern." So if we lack enough love to witness or we lack love while witnessing, we need to get on our knees and ask afresh for the help of God.

"Perhaps if there were more of that intense distress for souls that leads to tears, we should more frequently see the results we desire. Sometimes it may be that while we are complaining of the hardness of the hearts of those we are seeking to benefit, the hardness of our own hearts and our feeble apprehension of the solemn reality of eternal things may be the true cause of our want of success." —HUDSON TAYLOR

Too often our eyes are dry in prayer and that is reflected in our preaching. Catherine Booth said that if our listeners can't see tears in our eyes, they should hear tears in our voice.

One observer of George Whitefield said, "I could hardly bear such unreserved use of tears," for Whitefield was "frequently so overcome, that, for a few seconds, you would suspect he never could recover." Whitefield said of his tears, "You blame me for weeping, but how can I help it when you will not weep for yourselves, though your immortal souls are on the verge of destruction?"

Let us pray for a heart of compassion for the lost and love them enough to warn them of their fate.

CONTENDING OR CONTENTIOUS?

The Bible exhorts us to "contend earnestly for the faith" (Jude 1:3). As you are contending for the faith, of course you want to always make sure you are respectful, congenial, and uncompromising. But people won't stay and listen to boring preaching, so you have to be a bit "on the edge." Christians sometimes think that it's unloving to speak in such a way, but it is necessary if you want to hold your hearers. When I share the gospel with

The first time preaching on US soil (in Hawaii), in 1985. We need to preach with passion the message the world desperately needs to hear.

one or two people, there is an obvious gentleness in my tone. However, if you heard me preach in the open air, it may seem provocative or contentious. This is because if I preached the same way I speak, I would never hold a crowd. It is important in both cases that I am motivated by love, but if I don't keep the preaching "on the edge," I will lose my hearers in minutes (if not seconds).

Charles Spurgeon put it this way:

> In the streets a man must from beginning to end be intense, and for that very reason he must be condensed and concentrated in his thought and utterance.

This "intense" preaching may be misunderstood by those who don't know why it's there. The problem is that when we read the Gospels, we don't hear the passion involved in its discourses. When Jesus spoke, there were those in the crowd who hated Him and wanted to kill Him. People undoubtedly called out, accusing Him of blasphemy, or challenging Him with questions. The atmosphere likely would have been electric. That's the atmosphere that holds a crowd's attention. To become passive in the name of love and gentleness will pull the plug out and the electricity will immediately leave. (For more about Spurgeon's thoughts on open-air preaching, see appendix A.)

So be ready, because you may be accused of preaching without love. The accusations almost always come from those brethren who have never preached in the open air. When speaking of open-air preaching, R. A. Torrey said,

> Don't be soft. One of these nice, namby-pamby, sentimental sort of fellows in an open-air meeting, the crowd cannot and will not stand. The temptation to throw a brick or

a rotten apple at him is perfectly irresistible, and one can hardly blame the crowd.

Be sure to begin with an attitude of enthusiasm. The word means "in God," so let the fire of God touch your tongue. In other words, keep your energy level high. You are talking about everlasting life being a free gift from God, not about the secret life of elderly snails.

If others with you are also planning to speak, don't wind down after preaching the gospel. Keep your energy level high and hand it off to the next preacher. Introduce him and say that he is going to share something that is wonderful. If you wind down and say, "Well, thank you for listening folks," the crowd will leave and you'll scatter the incoming preacher's hearers.

"Catch on fire with enthusiasm and people will come for miles to watch you burn."

—JOHN WESLEY

To avoid burnout—especially when you're first beginning—don't go out and open-air preach for six hours and come back exhausted. Next week the thought of doing it again will become a burden. The reason I have been able to stick with it for so long is that it's not a physical burden. Preach for an hour or so, and don't feel bad about stopping. Remember the tortoise and the hare.

Most important, don't neglect to pray before you preach. Like Paul, pray for boldness to preach the gospel. Be prayerful while you are preaching, and pray after you preach, because

Jesus said that without Him we can do nothing. If He saw fit to pray all night, we need to pray all the time.

YOU CAN DO THIS!

Again, don't listen to your fears or discouraging thoughts. The time will come when your spirit will be willing but your flesh will be weak because you are old and feeble. Imagine sitting in a convalescent home, thinking about how you wasted your youth pursuing your own pleasures when people were going to Hell. We often apply the verse, "Remember now your Creator in the days of your youth" (Ecclesiastes 12:1) to the ungodly, when we should apply it to ourselves.

Always keep in mind that you will never be free from fear, especially just before you get up to speak in the open air. Overcome it through thoughts of the fate of the ungodly, the sacrifice of the cross, and the fact that God is watching you. Think of my friend who said that it was less fearful to skydive for the first time than to open-air evangelize, then consider the worst-case scenario if something goes wrong with both. In skydiving, if the parachute fails to open or becomes twisted, you fall to an unspeakably terrifying death. In open-air witnessing, you may make a fool of yourself and dent your ego. There is no comparison. So just do it, and God will be with you.

CHAPTER 3

BEARING THE REPROACH

*I was honored today with having a few stones,
dirt, rotten eggs, and pieces of dead cats
thrown at me.*

—GEORGE WHITEFIELD

H ave you noticed that the Bible is filled with "childish" stories that seem to insult the human intellect? There's a reason for that.

Years ago I ran a Bible club, and one day I told a large group of kids to line up for candy. As they did so, I noticed that it was a line of greed. The big bullies had pushed their way to the front, and the quiet, meek kids had been relegated to the back.

So I told them to turn around and face the other way. Then I took great delight in going to the other end of the line first.

That's what God has done with the ultimate gift of everlasting life. He turned the line around, and He did so by consistently using foolish things to confound the arrogant bullies of this world.

Who with any intellectual dignity would ever stoop to believe the childish stories of the Bible? The answer is: those who understand that in this world, where the rich get richer and the poor get stomped on, God has turned the line around.

The arrogant bullies of this world are the ultimate losers. God resists the proud and gives grace to the humble:

> Then Jesus called a little child to Him, set him in the midst of them, and said, "Assuredly, I say to you, unless you are converted and become as little children, you will by no means enter the kingdom of heaven." (Matthew 18:2–4)

God has been consistent with this principle—from Adam and Eve, to Noah and his ark, to Jonah and the great fish, to God being born into a human body in a cow shed, to the King of kings riding on a donkey, to the foolishness of preaching to save those who believe:

> "He has shown strength with His arm; He has scattered the proud in the imagination of their hearts. He has put down the mighty from their thrones, and exalted the lowly. He has filled the hungry with good things, and the rich He has sent away empty." (Luke 1:51–53)

You and I are called to preach a message in a manner that looks foolish to this God-hating world:

> For the message of the cross is foolishness to those who are perishing, but to us who are being saved it is the power of God...For since, in the wisdom of God, the world through wisdom did not know God, it pleased God through the foolishness of the message preached to save those who believe. (1 Corinthians 1:18,21)

So it's understandable that when you are preaching, you are going to attract the scorn of this world. One day I preached open air in the rain to about thirty people, who lined up outside the local courthouse. Most of them had umbrellas and as soon as I mentioned the things of God, a gentleman standing directly in front of me turned his back (and his umbrella) toward me. Many times I had preached to the back of people, but I could at least see the backs of their ears and felt that the sound had a chance of reaching them. But preaching to a big black umbrella was discouraging. It was a tragedy beyond words that the man was using an umbrella to shelter him from the gospel that told him how he could be sheltered from the terrible rain of God's wrath.

But there is a biblical evangelistic philosophy by which each of us should live. It is "Jesus was despised and rejected by men." That's the bottom line. If we live for Him, we too will be despised and rejected by men. Anything on top of that is a bonus. When He fed multitudes and healed the sick, they loved Him. But when He spoke of sin, righteousness, and judgment, they hated Him. Jesus said that He spoke of the world's evil deeds and that's why He was hated (John 7:7). He also said that if they hated Him, they will hate us. When you and I do what Jesus did, we shouldn't be surprised to get what Jesus got.

One man who witnesses wrote to say he's often called a bigot or "dead from the neck up," and said, "It's really discouraging." If you share this concern, this may help give you another perspective. Let me tell you about someone who opened up the Scriptures to his unsaved hearers. He told them that they hadn't kept the Commandments, and then he preached Jesus to them. Their reaction was a little negative also. They murdered him.

But someone was listening as he held the clothes of those who stoned Stephen to death. God, in His great wisdom, allowed that nightmare to happen for a reason.

May God forgive us for ever letting discouragement come near us. When we have faithfully planted the seed of His Word, it cannot return void. Our preaching and witnessing is never in vain. Ever.

> *"It is not our business to make the message acceptable, but to make it available. We are not to see that they like it, but that they get it."* —VANCE HAVNER

RESPONDING TO PERSECUTION

None of us like to be mocked as if we were intellectually lacking, or be hated or rejected by anyone. We crave acceptance. I'm continually mocked because I once suggested that the banana has design. Others took a quote from a book I wrote in 1978 out of context, falsely claiming I believed that "we should never see a doctor or take medicine, because we are interfering with the lesson that God is trying to teach us." Others made up quotes saying that I would rape and kill children if God told me to, and they put my name and photo with it, spreading it all over the Internet. So what should we do about these things? Jesus told us exactly how to handle it:

> "Blessed are you when men hate you, and when they exclude you, and revile you, and cast out your name as evil, for the Son of Man's sake. Rejoice in that day and leap for

joy! For indeed your reward is great in heaven, For in like manner their fathers did to the prophets." (Luke 6:22,23)

"Blessed are you when they revile and persecute you, and say all kinds of evil against you falsely for My sake. Rejoice and be exceedingly glad, for great is your reward in heaven, for so they persecuted the prophets who were before you." (Matthew 5:11,12)

We tend to think of God's blessing as a guarantee to a long life, health, and prosperity. But Jesus said we are also blessed if we are hated, disqualified, detested, persecuted, and if our very name is considered evil because we belong to Jesus. Then He said what we are to do to show that we believe we are blessed. We are to rejoice. We are to be exceedingly glad. And we are to leap for joy.

If you are living your life for Christ Jesus, you *will* suffer persecution (2 Timothy 3:12), and if you preach the gospel in the open air, you are *inviting* persecution. So when it comes, do what Jesus said to do. Don't get depressed or become discouraged; instead, rejoice. Thank God for the hatred. Praise Him for it, be exceedingly glad and then leap for joy. Jump off of this evil earth for a second or two. I do. You may not get far off the ground, but you will be showing God that you trust Him, and since we can't please God without faith, we please Him when we trust Him—and it's Heaven's smile that matters.

I have preached open air thousands of times and been beaten up only once. Although I have been mocked often, I really don't know the meaning of the word "persecution." Read *Foxe's Book of Martyrs* and I'm sure you will agree. Such freedoms in the US should make us want to double our efforts to reach the lost while we still have the liberty to do so.

> *"If Jesus had preached the same message that ministers preach today, He would never have been crucified."*
> —LEONARD RAVENHILL

Jesus also said, "You have heard that it was said, 'You shall love your neighbor and hate your enemy.' But I say to you, love your enemies, bless those who curse you, do good to those who hate you, and pray for those who spitefully use you and persecute you, that you may be sons of your Father in heaven; for He makes His sun rise on the evil and on the good, and sends rain on the just and on the unjust" (Matthew 5:43–45).

So after an atheist claimed I would rape and kill children if God told me to, and I continually received abuse from people asking how I could say such a thing, we had our lawyers trace the source and found that it was a Chicago businessman in his fifties. We had his name and address and enough evidence to consider a lawsuit. Instead, I send him a huge box of fresh cookies for him and his family, wishing them well. While some could certainly justify a lawsuit so that this wicked man would think twice before he slandered other ministries, I chose to take the easy path by giving it to God and rejoicing. A lawsuit would cause me to lose sleep. Showing kindness to nasty people makes me smile.

A PREACHER OF RIGHTEOUSNESS

The Bible tells us that Noah was "a preacher of righteousness" (2 Peter 2:5). However, we are not given further details about what he preached. This is because we don't need any. He was surrounded by wickedness and he preached righteousness, and righteousness naturally demands justice.

A preacher of righteousness puts others before himself. He is hated and mocked, but he sets that aside because love is the spring of his preaching. When I plead with the lost, I often tell them that I would rather be with my beautiful wife, but instead I'm with them because I care about where they spend eternity.

God had told Noah, "For after seven more days I will cause it to rain on the earth forty days and forty nights..." (Genesis 7:4). Noah knew that he had seven final days to preach, after which terrible judgment would come. It would be then that sinners would understand "the goodness and severity of God" (Romans 11:22). He had showered His goodness on them through the gift of life, but now God would rain on them the severity of His wrath because of their sin. Can you imagine the final thud of the ark door being closed? Can you hear the rumbling of distant thunder, and the dawning upon wicked minds that what Noah had been preaching was true? After those seven final days, Noah had only seven converts, and the door of grace was closed.

"What can be wiser than in the highest sense to bless our fellow men—to snatch a soul from the gulf that yawns, to lift it up to the heaven that glorifies, to deliver an immortal from the thralldom of Satan, and to bring him into the liberty of Christ?" —CHARLES SPURGEON

The moment is nearing for this world when God shuts the door of grace, and then will come the Judgment. So be like Noah and be a preacher of righteousness. Let thoughts of the fate of sinners spur you on to uphold the righteousness of the Law of God—a topic we will look at in the next chapter. Plead with the world about sin, righteousness, and judgment to come. The ark is waiting. The Door of the Savior is still open. Whosoever will may come. "Knowing, therefore, the terror of the Lord, we persuade men" (2 Corinthians 5:11).

CHAPTER 4

A UNIVERSAL MESSAGE

I do not believe that any man can preach the gospel who does not preach the Law. The Law is the needle, and you cannot draw the silken thread of the gospel through a man's heart unless you first send the needle of the Law to make way for it.

—CHARLES SPURGEON

I have shared the gospel with people of all colors, shapes, and sizes, Jews and Gentiles, and I find that although we must be culturally sensitive, they all react the same way to the same gospel when it's presented biblically. That's why I took a team and a camera crew to Europe and preached the gospel in thirteen countries in thirteen days and filmed the preaching for Season Four of our TV program. I wanted to expel the myth that before you can preach the gospel to the Chinese, Africans, or Russians, you have to learn the language, dress like them, eat their food, and "earn the right" to share the gospel with them.

All you need to reach people anywhere is a love that will swallow your fears and a good interpreter. You simply take people through the Ten Commandments as Jesus did, as Paul did, as James and the other apostles did, as did Whitefield, Wesley, Edwards, and Spurgeon, then you preach the glorious gospel. We cannot expect results if we plant seed on unplowed ground. The moral Law breaks up fallow ground. We cannot convince a patient to take a cure until we first convince him of the disease. The Law shows him that he has the fatal disease of sin. We'll be examining its place in evangelism in this chapter.

OFFICERS OF THE LAW

In 1982 (just after I had discovered the function of God's Law in evangelism) I was in my car in New Zealand looking for a photo processing place when I saw it across the street. There was a problem, though. The building was to my left, up a one-way street; I would have to go around the block to get to it. Or I could cut across the bottom of the one-way street and save time. So that's what I did.

As I was parking my car, I noticed a police officer parking his bike across the road. I mumbled, "He's not interested in me," grabbed the negatives, and ran up the stairs of the photo processing business. As I entered their lobby, I noticed that I had the wrong set of negatives in my hand so I turned around and headed back to the parking lot. The scene I saw was almost comical. The officer was casually leaning against my car. He knew it was just a matter of time until I'd be back.

He said, "May I see your driver's license, please?" As I handed it to him, he said something that shook me. He asked, "Have you any excuse for going the wrong way up a one-way street?" Huh? Going the wrong way up a one-way street? In my mind I had just cut across the corner (though I did have to drive slightly along the sidewalk to get to the parking lot). However, the law isn't interested in the angle in which I drove. I sat there wide-eyed and heard my mind say, "Guilty, guilty, guilty!" I looked the officer in the eye and replied, "No excuse whatsoever."

He thought for a moment. Then he said, "Well, there was no traffic coming. No harm was done, and I don't think you will do it again." His eye twinkled; he closed my license, handed it back to me, and walked away. I sat there, stunned, and breathed out a deep sigh.

That officer of the law had within his authority the discretion to show me mercy or justice, and he was looking for something in particular to make the decision about which way he would go. He was looking for "contrition"—sorrow of heart for violation of the law—and that would be evidenced by what came out of my mouth. If I had said, "Officer, it wasn't a serious transgression. I just cut across the bottom of the street. Besides, there are plenty of drivers worse than me," he would have thrown the book at me. But when he saw that my mouth was stopped—that I had no excuse whatsoever—he could see that I was truly sorry and that I wouldn't do it again. That showed him that mercy was called for.

We too are officers of the Law—God's moral Law—and we have within our authority to show mercy or judgment to criminals who stand before us. If they try to justify their sins, saying things like, "I've only told little white lies. I'm really a good person. There are plenty of people worse than me," then there's no sorrow for sin. They haven't seen the depth of their transgression, so we need to take courage and throw the Book at them and center on sin, righteousness, and judgment to come (Acts 20:24,25). We must, like Paul did with Felix, make them tremble.

> *"It is impossible for a person to fully realize his need for God's grace until he sees how terribly he has failed the standards of God's Law. It is impossible for him to realize his need for mercy until he realizes the magnitude of his guilt."*
>
> —JOHN MACARTHUR

MAKE THE BULLET HIT THE TARGET

It is obvious from Scripture that God requires us not only to preach to sinners, but also to teach them. The servant of the Lord must be "able to teach, patient, in humility correcting" those who oppose them (2 Timothy 2:24,25). For a long while I thought I was to leap among sinners, scatter the seed, then leave. But our responsibility goes further. We are to bring the sinner to a point of understanding his need before God. Psalm 25:8 says, "Good and upright is the LORD; therefore He teaches sinners in the way." Psalm 51:13 adds, "Then I will teach transgressors Your ways, and sinners shall be converted to You." The Great Commission is to teach sinners: "make disciples of all the nations ... teaching them to observe all things" (Matthew 28:19,20). The disciples obeyed the command, as "daily in the temple, and in every house, they did not cease teaching and preaching Jesus as the Christ" (Acts 5:42).

Some preachers are like a loud gun that misses the target. It may sound effective, but if the bullet misses the target, the exercise is in vain. He may be the largest-lunged, pulpit-pounding preacher this side of the Book of Acts. He may have great teaching on faith, but if the sinner leaves the meeting failing to understand his desperate need of God's forgiveness, then the preacher has failed. He has missed the target, which is the understanding of the sinner. Sinners will not flee from the wrath to come until they understand that they are guilty and under condemnation.

This is why the Law of God must be used in preaching. It teaches and instructs. The Law serves as a "tutor" to bring sinners to Christ (Galatians 3:24). A sinner will come to "know His will, and approve the things that are excellent," if he is "instructed out of the Law" (Romans 2:18).

In the parable of the sower, the "good-soil" hearer is he who "hears the word and understands it" (Matthew 13:23). Perhaps this is why Philip the evangelist saw fit to ask his potential convert, the Ethiopian eunuch, "Do you understand what you are reading?" (Acts 8:30).

This understanding seems to refer not only to sin, but also to the gospel. In the parable of the sower, the enemy is able to snatch the good seed from the wayside hearer because he lacks understanding. He doesn't understand that it is the message of everlasting life, so he gives it no value: "When anyone hears the word of the kingdom, and does not understand it, then the wicked one comes and snatches away what was sown in his heart" (Matthew 13:19).

My great desire is for sinners to understand the gospel and be saved. Although God alone saves the sinner, from the sowing to the reaping, I believe that, as a preacher of the gospel, my job is to strive (with the help of God) to bring about *understanding*. So rather than using "persuasive words of human wisdom" (1 Corinthians 2:4), I keep the message simple in the hope that the sinner will grasp what I am trying to say.

My gospel presentation may begin with a parable about a man stealing another man's lamb (as with Nathan and David), or with a quote by Athenian poets (as with Paul when he preached in Athens). I may use metaphors, similes, statistics, quotes, personal experiences, and of course I present the Law, the gospel, and the necessity of repentance and faith.

Incorporating the Law into the gospel presentation does many things. It primarily brings the knowledge of sin (see Romans 7:7), showing the sinner that he is a criminal and that God is his Judge. The Law (in the hand of the Holy Spirit) stops his mouth of justification and leaves him guilty before God (see Romans 3:19,20). It reveals that he deserves nothing but judgment for his crimes. Like a faithful prosecutor, the Law of God points its accusing finger, and so the sinner's stirred conscience bears witness and likewise points its finger at the criminal (see Romans 2:15). The verdict is "guilty," and the condemnation is just. I do my best to put him in the courtroom on the Day of Judgment, with the hope that he will understand the mercy that God offers him in Christ.

I may equate repentance to a criminal who becomes law-abiding and shows his sincerity by returning stolen goods. I perhaps will explain saving faith by differentiating it from an intellectual belief, and likening it to trusting a pilot or a parachute. I speak of the cross by explaining that it's like a civil judge paying a criminal's fine, thus satisfying the law and at the same time extending mercy. All these things are aimed at (with the help of God) bringing understanding to the sinner. If he doesn't understand the gospel, he won't value it and seek the Savior.

I then explain, "It was a legal transaction. You broke God's Law (the Ten Commandments), and Jesus paid your fine in His life's blood. That means that God can legally dismiss your case. You can leave the courtroom on the Day of Judgment because your fine has been paid. Does that make sense?"

Again and again, I can see the light go on in the eyes of my hearers. Many suddenly understand the gospel when I explain it that way. While this is certainly not a magic formula, I can say that legality is the essence of the cross. It was God's love for justice, and for guilty sinners, that drove Him to Calvary.

Man is unique among God's creation. He is forensic by nature. He intuitively understands the principles of law, retribution, justice, and mercy, because he is made in the image of God. That's why every civilization sets up court systems and why the moral Law resonates with a sinner's conscience. Scripture tells us that all mankind has "the work of the law written in their hearts, their conscience also bearing witness, and between themselves their thoughts accusing or else excusing them" (Romans 2:15). So when Paul uses the Law to bring the knowledge of sin to his hearers, he knows that it will find reverberation in their hearts:

> You, therefore, who teach another, do you not teach yourself? You who preach that a man should not steal, do you steal? You who say, "Do not commit adultery," do you commit adultery? You who abhor idols, do you rob temples? You who make your boast in the law, do you dishonor God through breaking the law? For "the name of God is blas-

phemed among the Gentiles because of you," as it is written. (Romans 2:21–24)

God is the "habitation of justice" (Jeremiah 50:7). We are guilty criminals. Our fine has been paid, and upon our repentance and faith in Jesus, we can leave the courtroom. Carefully explaining the gospel message, using legal vernacular to those whose understanding is "darkened," sheds new light on what they perceived to be just an old and irrelevant story.

> *"When 100 years ago earnest scholars decreed that the Law had no relationship to the preaching of the gospel, they deprived the Holy Spirit in the area where their influence prevailed of the only instrument with which He had ever armed Himself to prepare sinners for grace."*
> —PARIS REIDHEAD

THE "WONDERFUL PLAN" MESSAGE

In contrast, many sincere believers use the popular "God has a wonderful plan" message as a hook to get "decisions" for Christ. If you're unaware of the errors of this modern approach to the gospel, please consider the following thoughts:

1. You have been asked to preach the gospel to a thousand people on the 100th floor of the World Trade Center on September 10, 2001. You know that within twenty-four hours every one of them will die in ways that defy the imagination. Some will be burned alive with jet fuel. Others will jump one hundred stories to the unforgiving sidewalks of

New York, and the rest will fall with the building and be so crushed that their bodies will never be recovered. Are you going to talk about a wonderful plan? To do so would be to misrepresent the gospel. Instead you should speak of sin, righteousness, and judgment to come, as did the apostles.

2. There isn't a single Bible verse where the "wonderful plan" message is preached. (The "abundant" life spoken of by Jesus in John 10:10 simply means "full." Paul certainly had a full life. Jesus told him that he would suffer, and he truly had a life full of beatings, stonings, shipwreck, imprisonment, and martyrdom.)

3. Read *Foxe's Book of Martyrs* and see how the foundation of the Church is soaked in blood.

4. Take the time to freely read the book *God Has a Wonderful Plan for Your Life: The Myth of the Modern Message* and see the unspeakable damage that's been done by that "wonderful plan" message (freeWonderfulBook.com).

5. Try to reconcile the wonderful-plan message with verses about men killing you (thinking they are doing God a favor), being hated for His name's sake, entering the kingdom of God "through much tribulation," and persecution being promised to "all who desire to live godly in Christ Jesus."

6. Study how the Pharisees preferred to cling to their tradition over the truth of Scripture, and then think about how we are no different with our man-made methods of altar calls, the "sinner's prayer," emotive music to get decisions, and promises of an unbiblical wonderful plan. By clinging to tradition, we have filled the contemporary Church with false

converts. May God forgive us, and help us. (For more on false converts, see chapter 9.)

So if you are going to preach the gospel, make sure you prepare the soil biblically. You are speaking to criminals—those who have broken God's moral Law. God is willing to let them come to Christ for mercy so they may live, but they must understand the gravity of their transgressions against God.

> "The first use of [the Law], without question, is to convince the world of sin. By this is the sinner discovered to himself. All his fig-leaves are torn away, and he sees that he is 'wretched and poor and miserable, blind and naked.'"
> —JOHN WESLEY

On Judgment Day, the ungodly will have no one to blame but themselves. It's their own sin that will condemn them—not God's supposed sins, not Adam's, nor the sins of the hypocrites who sit in church. To add to their anguish will be the knowledge that God offered them forgiveness and they refused it:

> But in accordance with your hardness and your impenitent heart you are treasuring up for yourself wrath in the day of wrath and revelation of the righteous judgment of God, who "will render to each one according to his deeds": eternal life to those who by patient continuance in doing good seek for glory, honor, and immortality; but to those who are self-seeking and do not obey the truth, but obey unrighteousness—indignation and wrath, tribulation and anguish, on every soul of man who does evil... (Romans 2:5–9)

Years ago, a television advertisement had a deep-voiced commentator ask the sobering question, "What goes through the mind of a driver at the moment of impact in a head-on collision if he's not wearing a seatbelt?" As he spoke, the commercial showed a crash dummy without a safety belt, reacting in slow motion to a head-on collision. As the dummy moved forward with the impact, the steering wheel went right through its skull. Then the commentator somberly continued, "The steering wheel. You can learn a lot from a dummy. Buckle up!"

Why would they use such horrible "fear tactics"? The reason is clear: they were speaking the truth. It is a fearful thing to be in a head-on collision when you're not wearing a seatbelt.

Our sobering message is the gospel truth. The Bible warns, "It is a fearful thing to fall into the hands of the living God" (Hebrews 10:31). It is right that sinners should fear, because they are in danger of terrible eternal damnation. They are going to collide head-on with God's moral Law. Never hesitate to let Judgment Day play out before their eyes in slow motion so that they will soberly consider their need of the Savior.

> *"How shall I feel at the judgment, if multitudes of missed opportunities pass before me in full review, and all my excuses prove to be disguises of my cowardice and pride?"*
> —W. E. SANGSTER

THE KNOWLEDGE OF SIN

Francis Bacon's maxim "knowledge is power" can be a little confusing when coupled with "ignorance is bliss." Knowledge can be more than power and ignorance of certain things can kill you.

The Bible says that God's people were destroyed through a lack of knowledge of His Law (Hosea 4:6). Those who don't have knowledge of the moral Law don't have a knowledge of sin: Paul said, "I would not have known sin except through the law" (Romans 7:7), and "by the law is the knowledge of sin" (Romans 3:20). And if there no knowledge of sin, there is no repentance, without which sinners will perish (see Luke 13:1–3). (See chapter 8 for a discussion of repentance.)

The Law puts us in a dry desert of hopelessness, but in doing so it does us a great service. It gives us the knowledge that we can't save ourselves. It turns our head to God's mercy, which then pours down on us like a life-saving waterfall.

> "When once God the Holy Spirit applies the Law to the conscience, secret sins are dragged to light, little sins are magnified to their true size, and things apparently harmless become exceedingly sinful...[They] appear in their true color, as breaches of the Law of God, deserving condign punishment." —CHARLES SPURGEON

It prepares us for the greatest knowledge that any human being can ever attain: that the free gift of God is eternal life through Jesus Christ (Romans 6:23).

When we take someone through God's Law (whether in open-air preaching or personal witnessing), we are looking for contrition—just as the police officer was when I broke the law.

Is the person sorry for breaking the Commandments? Has he been humbled by the Law? Does he see the seriousness of his sin? Or is he still proud, proclaiming his innocence? Does he justify himself by saying he told only little white lies and there are plenty of people worse than him? Then he isn't sorry for his sins. We must therefore take courage, throw the Book at him, and with a God-given authority speak of sin, righteousness, and judgment to come, until he (like Felix) trembles because of his sin.

However, if his mouth is stopped (which is the purpose of the Law—see Romans 3:19,20) and he has no excuse whatsoever, then he has godly sorrow that produces repentance (2 Corinthians 7:10). The Bible says that mercy rejoices over judgment, so shut the book of the Law and give him mercy. With a sparkle in our eye, we can tell him of the incredible love of God, expressed in the wondrous cross on which the Prince of Glory died. God resists the proud, but gives grace to the humble (James 4:6), so use the Law to humble a proud person, and offer grace to those who have been humbled by the Law.

Here is the difference between open-air preaching and witnessing to an individual. You share the good news of salvation with the person you're speaking to, even if he lacks contrition. This is because you are preaching not only to him, but also to the many others who are listening, some of whom may be thinking, *What must I do to be saved?* You can do this by saying, "Fred, I know you aren't concerned about where you will spend eternity, but I am. You seem like a nice guy and I don't want you to end up in Hell. God sent His Son, Jesus, to suffer and die on the cross…," etc.

By incorporating the Commandments into our evangelistic message, using the Law to bring the knowledge of sin, we're now ready to share the gospel biblically. But before addressing our listeners, in the next chapter we'll look at how to prepare an open-air setting for maximum effectiveness.

CHAPTER 5

PREPARING YOUR SETTING

It would be very easy to prove that revivals of religion have usually been accompanied, if not caused, by a considerable amount of preaching out of doors, or in unusual places.

—CHARLES SPURGEON

There is a significant difference between messages preached in the open air and those preached in a building where people are sitting and attentive. People in a church building are there willingly and are a captive audience. In the open air, if people don't like what you are saying or think you are boring, they leave. Therefore, you need to learn the skills of open-air evangelism. The analogy of "fishing" for men is so applicable. A good fisherman is a skilled fisherman, and his skill comes by experience. He learns to go where the fish gather. He knows that seagulls gather where the fish are, or that certain seaweeds attract certain fish. He knows how to bait a hook so that it is disguised. He knows when to reel in the catch, and so on. These skills come by experience, but to hasten that experience for you, this chapter covers suggestions on how to choose a suitable "fishing hole" and how to create an orderly setting that's beneficial to both you and your audience.

CHOOSING A LOCATION

As they say with real estate, the most important consideration is "location, location, location." If you want to be a fisher of men, you have to go where the fish are. They don't come to you; you have to go to them.

A good open-air setting is any public location where people gather where they're not in a hurry and can take time to listen: beaches, parks (including skate parks), sports arenas, outside bars or music venues, near bus or train stops, farmer's markets, swap meets, fairs and festivals, outside courts or movie theaters, or anywhere people are waiting in line. Select a place that has plenty of foot traffic, where you will have a steady supply of people to hear the gospel, and away from the noise of the street, fountains, loud music, or machinery. It is ideal to have somewhere that will acoustically enhance your voice, such as near buildings, where the sound will bounce off and help amplify your preaching. Facing a hill or raised area will create a natural amphitheater, and having your back to any wind will enable your words to be carried further.

During the day, try to avoid areas where either you or your audience are having to squint into the sun. When preaching at night, of course, be careful to avoid high crime areas and stay in areas that are well lit. You shouldn't have problems speaking in public places in the United States; it is your First Amendment right to speak on American soil.

As noted earlier, my regular preaching spots have included open squares where lunch crowds gather, parks when the homeless congregate, crowded beaches, popular malls, and in front of courts—and on one occasion even the inside of a grocery store. Kirk Cameron and I had a seminar in Houston and planned to take a team and preach open air. About two hundred people registered for the open air. As we made our way out the door, it began to rain. Fortunately, our host had made provision for rain. He had permission from the owners of a supermarket to conduct the open air in the fruit and nut section of their store.

To our delight, that's what happened. I stood up in the huge modern supermarket on a plastic milk container and preached the gospel to the large crowd that gathered. Then Kirk also stood up and preached. It was an amazing and fruitful experience. So be creative; you never know what might happen.

I typically keep going back to the same area as long as people will listen to the gospel. This is because it is good for regulars to hear the gospel more than once. Try to remember their names and greet them when you see them. You will find that you can befriend these people, and some may even seek you out with questions. Another reason I stick with the same place is because of the old adage, "If it's not broke, why fix it?" This is also true when you find an effective fishing hole for handing out tracts and witnessing.

College campuses are wonderful places to witness because there are often large groups of students sitting between classes or gathering in common areas for lunch. Young people are often more open to discuss the things of God than those who have become hardened in their philosophies. Also keep in mind that you will be speaking to future doctors, lawyers, and politicians—society's leaders, those who could greatly influence the future. Just one word from you that God uses could change many lives. If you don't bother to reach out to them they will become steeped in the errors of humanism, atheism, and evolution. So take courage—call or go to your local college or university, tell them you'd like to come and speak, and ask for their requirements. They may let you speak with or without amplification. You may need some sort of insurance, or they may want to restrict you to a certain area. If there is a Christian organization on the campus that invites you, that usually gets around any red tape.

"We ought actually to go into the streets and lanes and highways, for there are lurkers in the hedges, tramps on the highway, streetwalkers, and lane haunters whom we shall never reach unless we pursue them into their own domains."
—CHARLES SPURGEON

CHALK IT UP

Before beginning an open-air session, I draw a chalk line in an arc in front of my "soapbox" (being sure to remove it before I leave). I use a piece of string tied to my soapbox so that the line is curved. You could also place some colorful masking tape in a semi-circle. This helps with both crowd formation and control.

A reasonably close, orderly crowd is more attractive to potential listeners. If someone walks by and sees a straggly group, they are less likely to stop and listen. But if a large group of people is standing four or five deep, listening to someone speak, it has the effect of giving instant credibility to the speaker—pulling in even more listeners. Their curiosity will often draw them in.

Depending on your location, a good distance for the chalk line is about 15 feet away. If it's too close, you can't raise your voice so more people can hear the gospel, and if it's too distant, you can't be heard.

When people stop to listen, you can have them move up closer to the chalk line. To do this say that you went to great expense and trouble to draw the line and ask them, "Could you do me a big favor? To save my voice, could you step up to this line? It will also mean that I don't have to 'yell' at you to be heard (which sounds rude and unloving). Thank you." And people do what you ask, if you ask politely but firmly. This will not only help your voice, but it will help to draw others to hear the gospel—because a crowd draws a crowd.

You can also ask people to move back behind the chalk line if they get too close, which can quench the preaching. Sometimes people just stand there, so you may like to firmly say, "We're not going for the big money until people come up to the line" (referring to giving away prizes to anyone who proves to be a good person; how to do this is described later).

The picture below was taken in October 2012 at UC Berkeley—the bastion of godless liberalism. Despite its dubious reputation, university authorities kindly gave us a four-hour permit to share the gospel with amplification. They even allowed us to film. To create the orderly, attentive crowd, we simply drew a circular chalk line and respectfully asked the crowd to remain behind the line, which they did. Additional attentive listeners were standing on balconies and sitting on steps.

During an open air at UC Berkeley, a chalk line helps to keep the listeners orderly.

CROWD ETIQUETTE

When you are just beginning, bring someone with you who has done open-air preaching before. If you can't find someone, ask a couple of friends to come with you so they can give you feedback afterwards. In fact, the more laborers there are, the better. R. A. Torrey stated, "Get as large a number of reliable Christian men and women to go with you as you possibly can. Crowds draw crowds. There is great power in numbers. One man can go out on the street alone and hold a meeting; I have done it myself; but if I can get fifteen or twenty reliable men to go with me, I will get them every time." So if you can, bring several other Christians with you and have them form an audience and look as though they are listening to your preaching. This will encourage others to stop and listen. Just make sure that your helpers never stand with their back to you or distract your listeners while you're speaking. Ask them to pay attention.

I have seen open-air meetings when a fellow laborer is sharing the gospel, and what are the Christians doing? They are talking among themselves. Why then should anyone stop and listen if those right in front of the speaker aren't even attentive? It is so easy to chat with friends when you've heard the gospel a million times before. I have found myself doing it, but it is so disheartening for the preacher to speak to the backs of a crowd. Aside from serving as attentive crowd members, fellow Christians can be praying during the preaching, both for the preacher and for the listeners.

Also, instruct Christians not to argue with hecklers. Hecklers are folks who verbally disagree with what you say. The best thing that can happen to an open-air meeting is to have a good heckler. Jesus gave us some of the greatest gems of Scripture because someone either made a statement or asked a question in an open-air setting.

A good heckler can increase a crowd of twenty people to two hundred in a matter of minutes. The air becomes electric and you suddenly have two hundred people listening intently to how you will answer a heckler. All you have to do is remember the attributes of 2 Timothy 2:24–26: be patient, gentle, humble, and so on. However, if other Christians argue with the heckler, that will ruin an open-air meeting. I have seen an old lady hit a heckler with her umbrella and turn the crowd from listening to the gospel to watching the fight she has just started. Who can blame them? Remember, the enemy will do everything he can to distract your listeners. Don't let him.

As listeners peel away from the crowd, instruct your helpers to follow them and either try to engage them in conversation (away from where you're speaking) or offer them a tract. This will give everyone who stops to listen an opportunity to hear the gospel.

GIVE YOURSELF A LIFT

Another important point when preaching in the open air is to elevate yourself. This serves several purposes. First, it will help you gain attention. When I first started preaching back in 1974, for eighteen months I preached without any elevation and hardly attracted any listeners. As soon as I got a "soapbox" to stand on, people stopped to listen. Their attitude was, "What has this guy got to say?" They had an excuse to stop.

Also, elevation will give you protection. I was once almost eaten by an angry 6'6" gentleman who kept fuming, "God is love!" We were eye to eye...while I was elevated. On another occasion, a very heavy gentleman who had a mean countenance placed it about 6" from mine and whispered, "Jesus said to love your enemies." I nodded in agreement. Then he asked in a deep voice, "Who is your enemy?" I shrugged. His voice deepened and spilled forth in a chilling tone, *"Lucifer!"* I was standing beside my stepladder at the time so he pushed me backward with his stomach. He kept doing it again and again until I was moved back about 20 feet. I prayed for wisdom then said, "You are either going to hit me or hug me." He hugged me and walked off. That wouldn't have happened if I had been elevated.

Hecklers will often be offended by the fact that you are elevated. They will say things like, "Why are you standing on that box? Do you think you are better than the rest of us?" I usually say that I'm on a box because I'm short, and will get off for a moment to make the point. That makes the crowd laugh and defuses the anger. However, if you aren't short, you will have to say something like you are elevated so that people at the back can hear your voice.

R. A. Torrey said, "Take your own position a little above the part of the audience nearest you, upon a curbstone, chair, platform, rise in the ground, or anything that will raise your head above others so that your voice will carry."

"We must school and train ourselves to deal personally with the unconverted. We must not excuse ourselves, but force ourselves to the irksome task until it becomes easy."
—CHARLES SPURGEON

Elevation will also give you added authority. Hecklers will sometimes walk right up to you and ask questions quietly. This is usually an attempt to stifle the preaching, and it will work if you are not higher than your heckler. If they come too close to me, because I am higher I talk over their heads and tell them to go back to the heckler's gallery, and they usually obey me because they get the impression I am bigger than they are.

When Ezra preached the Law, he was elevated (Nehemiah 8:4,5). John Wesley used elevation to preach. Jesus preached the greatest sermon ever on a mount (Matthew 5–7), and Paul went up Mars Hill to preach (Acts 17:22). So if you can't find a hill-

In 2006 in Times Square, New York City, I was preaching from a plastic milk crate when two police officers told me that I could speak to the crowd but wasn't allowed to stand on the milk crate. It was very strange. Elevation is vital when it comes to open-air preaching, so two kind and humble Christian brothers who knew this (and had a sense of humor) gave me a lift.

top to preach from, use a soapbox or a stepladder. A "soapbox" is synonymous with open-air speaking, but nowadays laundry soap often comes in cardboard boxes. So it's best to look for alternatives such as extra sturdy step stools, or a "tool case" type (not a fold-up option) that can be found in most hardware stores.

We not only have our own preacher's soapbox, we have one for the heckler. This will stop the impression that the preacher is being judgmental and looking down upon the person to whom he is speaking. Having the heckler on his own soapbox also helps to attract more people to the crowd. Strangers who are walking by can see two people who are above the height of the crowd having a discussion. This often draws them in to hear what is being said.

Most places in the US allow public speaking when there is no amplification. It is best to check your city's requirements when it comes to using amplification; they vary from city to city. For areas that allow amplification, I would recommend that you don't buy a portable amp that's too low cost as it will distort your voice, and be sure to check online reviews before buying.

We also set up a microphone for hecklers, so they could be heard when they objected to the gospel. Unknown to them, there was a switch under my foot, and if they cussed, I would turn their microphone off. Then I would say, "That microphone switches off if you cuss. If you say that you are sorry and won't do it again, it will come back on." It was amusing to see the person tap the microphone, realize that it was turned off, and quickly apologize to the crowd. It was a great way to maintain control.

*Having soapboxes for both the preacher and the heckler
will attract more people.*

YOUR BACKDROP

Some open-air preachers may choose to surround themselves
with signs containing Bible verses, or carry a cross, or hold a
Bible. There are no hard-and-fast rules when it comes to the
public proclamation of the gospel, and you should do whatever
you think works best for you.

However, the Bible tells us that sinners hate the light (John
3:20). So I don't post gospel texts around where I preach, or
even hold a Bible while I'm preaching. I don't want people to
have a prejudicial attitude toward the gospel.

We are not living in the days of John Wesley, George White-field, and Charles Spurgeon, when there was a measure of respect for the Bible and for men of God. We are living in a time when the Scriptures are mocked as being anti-science, and where Christians are often vilified by the secular media as narrow-minded bigots. Those in the media have no lack of material with which to malign us. Modern evangelism has filled the church with many false converts, and they are often the ones who make it onto the news. They carry signs with condemning Bible verses, or they protest at soldiers' funerals with signs proclaiming God hates certain groups of people. This has created a stereotype of Christians in the minds of the secular world, so when they see us holding signs or carrying Bibles as we begin to speak, we have a mountain of prejudice to climb before we even present the message.

In the same way, we want to avoid causing offense by what we wear. It sounds a little strange, but even if I'm preaching at the beach, I try to wear clothing that is both modest and matches the environment. I don't wear an unbuttoned shirt unless I'm wearing a T-shirt underneath. I don't want to distract a listener by wearing any weird or inappropriate clothing.

There are other, more effective ways we can attract listeners to hear our message, and that's what we will look at in the next chapter.

CHAPTER 6

GETTING STARTED

*Preach abroad... It is the cooping yourselves up
in rooms that has dampened the work of God,
which never was and never will be carried out to
any purpose without going into the highways
and hedges and compelling men and
women to come in.*

—JONATHAN EDWARDS

As you get started in open-air evangelism, keep in mind that you are desperately needed to "go into the world and preach the gospel to every creature" (Mark 16:15). So don't listen to your fears; just do it. If you have ever felt the joy of sharing the gospel with someone who is genuinely listening to every word you are saying, multiply that by thirty. That's a good open-air session. There's nothing like it when you have a good heckler and a crowd of people listening to the words of everlasting life.

If you're fearful about testifying open-air for the first time, practice at home before doing it "live." Go over the gospel in your mind until it's second nature—no, until it's first nature. When you are alone, preach it. (In the shower is a great place to practice.) Go through a few anecdotes. Get used to the sound of your own voice. Watch yourself in front of a mirror, and record yourself and listen to how you sound. To pretend to engage a heckler, invite some friends over to role-play with you—and practice what you preach.

If you are afraid of looking foolish if you mentally draw a blank while speaking, have a backup plan. Keep a New Testament with you and if you freeze up say, "I would just like to read something to you." Read John 3:16–18 and conclude with, "Thank you for listening." Just knowing you have that option will dissipate the fear.

If someone asks you a question that you don't know how to answer, simply say, "I'm sorry, I don't know the answer to that, but I will try to find it for you if you really want to know." There's nothing wrong with a humble admission. In fact, it may speak volumes more to your hearers than an eloquent answer.

With Bible "difficulties," I regularly fall back on the powerful statement of Mark Twain: "Most people are bothered by those passages of Scripture they don't understand, but for me I have always noticed that the passages that bother me are those I do understand." So once you have said that you don't know the answer, get back to the person's responsibility toward God on Judgment Day, as Jesus did in Luke 12:1–3.

You are going to have fears, not only before you begin but also each time you do it (I still do). They will be so real that they'll make you sweat. But for the sake of the lost, don't listen to them; just do it. The suggestions in this chapter will help you to get started: to gather listeners, keep their attention, and preach the gospel effectively.

DRAWING A CROWD

We are living in a unique day. I remember looking back at some of the television programs I used to enjoy as a teenager, like *The Beverly Hillbillies* and *Get Smart*. I originally thought they were funny, but nowadays I find them embarrassingly corny. They hardly cause me to even smile. But those programs haven't changed; I have. I have become far more particular because (like most people today) I have been bombarded with entertainment for years, and if we don't see a car chase and a shootout within a few minutes, we are bored.

At the time of great open-air preachers, people weren't bombarded with entertainment, and so someone speaking in the open air attracted their eyes and ears. However, nowadays, someone speaking in public about religion doesn't attract a crowd as it once did. In fact, you and I would be hard pressed to get a handful of people to listen to the gospel. I know, because I have tried every means possible to pull in a crowd of listeners. Therefore we have to be as wise as serpents and as gentle as doves. A serpent gets its heart's desire subtly. Our desire is for sinners to gather under the sound of the gospel.

It's not enough for me to stand on a street corner, reading from the Bible and speaking to whoever passes by. I want people to listen and *understand* the gospel. Some speakers don't mind not having listeners. I want the lost to hear and turn around to avoid the damnation of Hell. So I have experimented over the years to find what works and what doesn't work...and for the last twenty-five years I have found something that works wonderfully, which I will share in the following pages.

One way to attract "fish" is to use any type of entertainment, such as playing a guitar and singing. If it would help me pull in a crowd, I would sing, if I could. If I could dance or juggle or smash wood with my fist, I would use that skill for the glory of God. If you have a talent of any sort, give serious consideration to using it to reach the lost. Some Christians have a great talent but set it aside, thinking that it was just part of their old, sinful life. Then resurrect it for the sake of the unsaved. If you can do sleight-of-hand (magic tricks), do it. Rekindle the skill.

However, make sure that any entertainment is used to attract people to the message, rather than distract them from it. If it continues while you're witnessing, people won't be listening to your words. So once you have their attention, stop the entertainment, but keep it handy, and do something else for your listeners when you have finished speaking to leave them with a positive note.

Another suggestion to draw and hold a crowd is to search the Internet for pictures of celebrities who have died. Print a large copy of each and staple them at the top left corner. Go through them one at a time, asking the crowd who they are and why they are famous (their most notable movie, etc.). Then ask what they all have in common.

As people call out their answers, watch for someone who is confident and loud. Ask for his name as you ask why the celebrity was famous, etc. Be sure you deliberately log his name into your memory. Call on him a couple of times and ask him for the identity of the next celebrity. In doing so you are building a

PREACHING DO'S AND DON'TS

In a nutshell, here are some general how-to tips to keep in mind when you begin.

DO:

- Do talk *to* people, not *at* them, or worse, down to them.

- Do speak in a lively, confident manner. Fire and energy will hold a crowd. Cold, tedious preaching will not.

- Do speak with the right tone. What you say to a crowd is just as important as how you say it. Let them hear the passion and concern in your voice. Find a tone that is loving but firm, gentle but bold, humble but uncompromising.

- Do find the right volume level for your voice. Speak loudly enough for people to hear you while still using a pleasant, conversational tone. Don't yell, scream, or strain your voice.

- Do speak from your stomach rather than from your throat. If you don't eat beforehand, you should end up with strained stomach muscles when you are done. This is a good sign that you are using your diaphragm to project your voice rather than your throat. If you solely use your throat, your voice may not last very long and you may do damage to your voice.

- Do use lots of illustrations and word pictures.

- Do expect some "street wit" (smart alecks or jokers in the crowd), and be prepared to answer. But respond with genuine wit, not sarcasm or humor that humiliates.

- Do be snappy and brief. If you dwell too long on any one point, you will lose your crowd. Speak intensely with short sentences and with simple, direct points. "The chain of thought must be taken to pieces, and each link melted down and turned into bullets" (Charles Spurgeon).

- Do be wise as a serpent but gentle as a dove (Matthew 10:16).

- Do remind your hearers of your motives. You don't want their money. You're not telling them to join a church. You are there only because you care about their eternal welfare.

DON'T:

- Don't be dull! Be energetic; use illustrations and humor.
- Don't read or use notes. Commit your message to memory.
- Don't talk too long. Ten minutes is often more than enough. Open-air crowds don't want to listen to a long-winded preacher. Be passionate but be brief!
- Don't ever lose your temper! When you get angry, your message looks weak. If you stay calm, your message looks strong.
- Don't let an angry listener shake you. Anger is often a response to conviction of sin. "If you throw a rock into a pack of dogs, the one who yelps is the one who got hit."

FINISHING UP:

- Always remember to politely thank the crowd for their time and attention.
- Hand out as many tracts as you can before the crowd disperses. Plant friends in the crowd to help with this.

AFTERWARD:

- If you had fellow Christians with you, ask them for feedback or suggestions.
- If you couldn't get a crowd or things didn't go well, don't be discouraged. Even the best preachers sometimes say the wrong thing or fail to draw a crowd. Use your mistakes as an opportunity to learn and grow. Failure keeps us humble, and a humble person is the one God most uses.
- Like any other skill, preaching only improves with practice.
- Remember that success is not determined by the number of converts, but by your faithfulness in proclaiming the gospel.

relationship so that you can come back to him (or a couple of other people you have befriended) and ask, "Bill, tell me—what are your thoughts on what happens after someone dies? Is there a Heaven? Is the person reincarnated? Do you think there is a Hell?" Then take him through the Commandments. (For how to do this, see "The 'Good Person' Test" later in the chapter.)

TRIVIA PURSUIT

I have found that a very effective way to build up a crowd is to ask trivia questions and give dollar bills to those who answer correctly—and even to those who get the answer wrong. Stuart Scott and I have been drawing a crowd this way for many years. I am not saying that every open-air preacher should imitate what I do; I am simply saying this has worked well for me.

> *"Oh my friends, we are loaded with countless church activities, while the real work of the church—that of evangelizing and winning the lost is almost entirely neglected."*
> —OSWALD J. SMITH

For example, simply offer $1 to anyone who can name ten beers. If someone names only five, give him a dollar "as a consolation prize." This creates good will with the crowd. Keep asking for other volunteers who can name ten. After that, offer $10 to anyone who can name all of the Ten Commandments, in order (very few can). That will get several people quoting the Commandments, making it easy for you to ask who has kept each one.

Then offer $20 to anyone who *proves* to be a good person. When taking someone through the Ten Commandments, appoint six people in the crowd to act as a jury (people are usually quick to judge the sins of others). That will help to engage the crowd, and it will take the heat off you. After giving the gospel it's good to say, "Thanks for being a good sport. You didn't prove to be a good person, so you don't get the $20. But I have something else for you. Here's $5 as a gift. You didn't earn it, but I'm giving it to you because I care for you. That's called 'grace.' God offers everlasting life as a gift to sinners, not because we earned it, but simply because of His amazing grace." Have the person come forward to receive the $5, then explain that it wasn't his until he received it. So it is with the gift of God.

"It is no marvel that the devil does not love field preaching! Neither do I; I love a commodious room, a soft cushion, a handsome pulpit. But where is my zeal if I do not trample all these underfoot in order to save one more soul?"
—JOHN WESLEY

It's important to ask trivia questions that anyone can answer. You don't want to use questions that are difficult to answer, because you want to give away money and create a sense of fun and excitement.

So often the church is accused of taking people's money. By giving away money, you not only can silence that criticism, but you can make people happy when you do so. When Christians ask me why I give away money, I tell them that Jesus often mentioned money when speaking to crowds. It is a way to get the world's attention. It's unusual. A preacher giving away money is unnatural—like water running uphill. Jesus said that the world will either love money or love God. So this speaks their language. For an example of offering cash prizes for trivia, go to LivingWaters.com/OAP and watch "Using Trivia for Cash."

WHY NOT JUST OPEN A BIBLE?

There are some in the church who look down on the use of trivia and giving away money as being unspiritual. It does seem more spiritual to simply open a Bible and preach from it. However, let's look at how Paul preached in Athens:

> Then Paul stood in the midst of the Areopagus and said, "Men of Athens, I perceive that in all things you are very religious; for as I was passing through and considering the objects of your worship, I even found an altar with this inscription:
>
> TO THE UNKNOWN GOD.
>
> Therefore, the One whom you worship without knowing, Him I proclaim to you: God, who made the world and everything in it, since He is Lord of heaven and earth, does not dwell in temples made with hands. Nor is He worshiped with men's hands, as though He needed anything, since He gives to all life, breath, and all things. And He has made from one blood every nation of men to dwell on all the face of the earth, and has determined their preappointed times and the boundaries of their dwellings, so that they should seek the Lord, in the hope that they might grope for Him and find Him, though He is not far from

each one of us; for in Him we live and move and have our being, as also some of your own poets have said, 'For we are also His offspring.' Therefore, since we are the offspring of God, we ought not to think that the Divine Nature is like gold or silver or stone, something shaped by art and man's devising. Truly, these times of ignorance God over-looked, but now commands all men everywhere to repent, because He has appointed a day on which He will judge the world in righteousness by the Man whom He has ordained. He has given assurance of this to all by raising Him from the dead." (Acts 17:22–31)

The reason Paul didn't open the New Testament and preach from it was because the New Testament hadn't yet been compiled. I doubt if he opened up the Old Testament because the printing press hadn't been invented, so there was no such thing as a Bible in book form. I also doubt that he opened up Old Testament scrolls and read from them. They were precious and were kept in the Temple. Though Paul frequently went to the Jewish synagogues on the Sabbath and "reasoned with them from the Scriptures" (Acts 17:1–3), when preaching to the general public, Paul used a different approach. In speaking on Mars Hill, he quoted secular godless Greek poets.

In addressing this, the *Jamieson-Fausset-Brown Bible Commentary* states:

> *For we are also his offspring*—the first half of the fifth line, word for word, of an astronomical poem of Aratus, a Greek countryman of the apostle, and his predecessor by about three centuries. But, as he hints, the same sentiment is to be found in other Greek poets.

Barnes' Notes on the Bible added:

As Paul was a native of the same country it is highly probable he was acquainted with his writings. Aratus passed much of his time at the court of Antigonus Gonatas, king of Macedonia. His principal work was the "Phoenomena," which is here quoted, and was so highly esteemed in Greece that many learned men wrote commentaries on it... *It is one instance among thousands where an acquaintance with profane learning may be of use to a minister of the gospel.* (emphasis added)

When Paul quoted secular poets, he was showing his hearers that he was familiar with Greek literature. Clearly, he did this as a bridge for them to hear the gospel—he had their attention because he was speaking their language.

So, if we want to capture the ears of a crowd, we should speak their language. We should take a moment to quote Greek poets. By that I mean, we should say something that will resonate with them. Millions love the humor of comedians who speak about things we can all identify with. Who of us hasn't entered a plane and felt condescension from snooty First Class passengers, who are already busy making money on their laptops, or stood behind a lone passenger as he tried to push his household furniture into the overhead compartment—with no concern that he was holding up a line of two hundred stressed passengers, who just want to get to their seats?

Resonance is our lifeblood whenever we address other human beings. We want to connect with our hearers, whether we're speaking to one or one hundred, and not just sound like an off-key trumpet blast. Greek poets helped Paul get in tune with the Athenians.

That's why we use trivia. People enjoy it and stay for the gospel. Some may label it as entertainment. So be it. I would rather use trivia and draw hearers who will listen to the gospel than look spiritual and talk to nobody, which so often happens with preachers holding a Bible.

You are trying to build a bridge to your hearers. You want to endear them to you rather than alienate them, for the gospel's sake, so attract them with interesting trivia and win them through kindness. Give away money when people get the answer right, and remember to give it away when they get an answer wrong. Hand out money to kids just for trying. I will often ask a child for his name. When he says, "Timmy," I say, "That's right!" and I give him a dollar. This makes the crowd laugh.

It's also helpful to have the crowd applaud enthusiastically when answers are given—even if they are incorrect. Say, "That was wrong, but it was a good try. Let's give him a hand!" Loud, enthusiastic applause draws more people to the crowd, so the more people clapping the better. Considering having a friend step forward at appropriate times with an "Applause!" sign and encourage everyone to clap.

TRIVIA QUESTIONS

A good set of trivia questions to ask is "capitals of the world." Again, don't make the questions difficult. You want anyone to be able to answer because you want to give away money. That's what will attract a crowd. So make them easy, such as "What is the capital of England, France, Japan, etc.?" Here are some more:

- Where was the Declaration of Independence signed? *(Along the bottom)*

- Who wrote, "Ask not what your country can do for you. Ask what you can do for your country"? *(President Kennedy's speechwriter)*

- What is the only fish that can blink with both eyes? *(A shark)*

- Who was John Lennon's first girlfriend? *(Thelma Pickles)*

- How long does it take the average person to fall asleep: 2 minutes, 7 minutes, or 4 hours? *(7 minutes)*

- How long is a goldfish's memory span: 3 seconds, 3 minutes, or 3 hours? *(3 seconds)*

- How many muscles does a cat have in each ear: 2, 32, or 426? *(32)*

- What is the dumbest domesticated animal? *(Turkey—not a husband)*

- What is the world's smallest bird? *(Hummingbird)*

- How many Commandments was Moses given? *(Ten)*

- How many can you name? *(This will give you a potential candidate for the "Good Person" test.)*

- How many dictionary definitions are there for the word "good"? *(Around forty-five)*

- What was Elvis Presley's first record label? *(Sun Records)*

- What are Latter-Day Saints otherwise known as? *(Mormons)*

- What do you call a puppet controlled by strings? *(Marionette)*

- Astraphobia is a fear of what? *(Lightning)*

- Which presidents' faces are sculpted on Mount Rushmore? *(Washington, Jefferson, Roosevelt, and Lincoln)*

- Where in the human body is the thyroid gland? *(Neck)*

- What insect lives in a formicary? *(Ant)*

- What is John F. Kennedy's middle name? *(Fitzgerald)*

- Which US city has the largest population? *(New York City)*

- What is the common name for nitrous oxide? *(Laughing gas)*

- What type of domestic cat has no tail? *(Manx)*

- What is the world's longest river? *(The Nile)*

While you are asking questions, keep an eye out for people with a strong personality. You are looking for someone in the crowd with a loud voice and who has confidence. Once your crowd has built, ask if anyone would like to go for $20. Explain that you are looking for someone who thinks they are a good person. Say this: "Hands up those of you who think you are a good person. Put your hand down if you are a Christian. I don't want Christians, I want good people." It is a dead end to take someone through the Commandments and find that they are genuinely saved. So you need to weed out those dear Christians who trust in Jesus, but think that they are morally good. Make sure you say this with a tongue-in-cheek tone. If hands are still raised say that you want someone with a loud voice.

If no one responds, go back to the trivia and try again a few minutes later as new people join the crowd.

The best way I have found to generate interest is to engage someone in conversation. Don't wait until someone heckles you or asks you a question—you ask them. Call on people who stop and listen. Say, "You, sir! Do you think that there's a Heaven? Why or why not? Do you think that you are a good person?" Keep at it until his initial shock of being "picked on" wears off. Some of the best hecklers I've had came from me prompting them. So be bold.

> *"Let eloquence be flung to the dogs rather than souls be lost. What we want is to win souls. They are not won by flowery speeches."* —CHARLES SPURGEON

Let's say the man's name is Eric. Say, "Eric, jump up on the box. Let's give Eric a big hand for having the courage to get on the box. Eric, thanks for being a good sport." You've said his name three times to lodge it into your memory because you don't want to forget it. When it you talk to him about his personal sins and where they will take him on Judgment Day, you want to keep it personal by using his name. Before you take him through the Commandments ask him where he lives and what he does for a job, using his name again as you do so. This shows that you genuinely care about him.

To avoid a misunderstanding, repeat what is about to take place. Just say, "Eric, here's the deal. If you prove to be a good person I will give you $20. If you don't, I will give you $5 and a free DVD as a consolation prize, and you will win a free trip for two to Hawaii at your own expense. So it's a win/win situation. Okay?"

It's important to repeat what you have said. This is because some nasty people in the crowd may demand that you give him $20 just for participating.

THE "GOOD PERSON" TEST

After Eric agrees to the conditions, take him through the Ten Commandments. Ask him how many lies he has told in his whole life. When he gives a number, ask him, "What do you call someone who tells lies?" This is very important, because you want to personalize his sins. The human mind is naturally delusional. We can detect sin in others but rarely in ourselves—not unlike with bad breath and body odor. The truth has to come from an objective source. You want to do what Paul did in Romans chapter 2, where he said, "You who preach that a man should not steal, do you steal? You who say, "Do not commit adultery," do you commit adultery?" (vv. 21,22).

With God's help you want Eric to realize the gravity of his sin and cry out, "God, be merciful to me a sinner!" (Luke 18:13). To do this you have to point out his personal sins. Like Nathan to the delusional King David, you have to say, "You are the man! ...Why have you despised the commandment of the LORD?" (2 Samuel 12:7,9). This will take courage on your part, but you can do it, and you can do it with love and gentleness. Remember, you have an ally right in the heart of the enemy: it's the sinner's conscience. It will bear witness with God's Law, as David's conscience did.

Make sure you have a sober tone as you are doing this. Sin is extremely serious, and you want him to understand the gravity of his actions. Most of the crowd and the person to whom you are speaking will think lightly of lying, stealing, using God's name in vain, and especially of lust. So your tone at this point must be very sober. Now and then you will get someone who refuses to acknowledge their sin. They will say that they have never lied, nor stolen, nor use God's name in vain, or looked with lust. This sort of person is usually trying to frustrate you.

So what I do in this situation is ask if he has kept the First of the Ten Commandments. If he says he has, I ask him what it is. He more than likely won't know. Then I explain that the First Commandment means to put God first. It means to love the One who gave you your life, with all of your heart, soul, mind, and strength. If he claims he has kept that Commandment, say that God's Word tells us there are none who seek after Him.

"The Law flashes conviction on every side. He feels himself a mere sinner. He has nothing to pay. His 'mouth is stopped' and he stands 'guilty before God.'" —JOHN WESLEY

Either he is lying, or God is lying, and it is impossible for God to lie (Hebrews 6:18). So now he has shown that he hasn't obeyed the First Commandment. He has broken that one, he has lied publicly (which makes him a liar), which means everything he has said in the past about him not sinning can't be trusted. He is also an idolater because he doesn't have a right understanding of God's character and nature, and that's enough sin to put him in big trouble on Judgment Day.

Again, even if you don't sense a conviction of sin from the individual you're addressing, when witnessing in the open air it's wise to go ahead and explain the gospel. It may seem like a contentious crowd, but there could be one or more individuals who are listening.

RECOMMENDED VIDEOS

Go to LivingWaters.com/OAP to watch the following clips:

EXCELLENT ANALOGY: "Bill Gates" Open-Air

START TO FINISH: Open-Air Paris

USING THE IQ TEST: Huntington Beach Open-Air #18

MAKES A COMMITMENT: Huntington Beach Open-Air #12

REASONING WITH SINNERS: Huntington Beach Open-Air #6

OTHER SUGGESTIONS

To gather a crowd, you can catch people's attention by asking passersby what they think is the greatest killer of drivers in the US. This stirs curiosity. Someone may call out "Alcohol!" or "Falling asleep at the wheel!" Say that it's not and repeat the question a few more times, adding that you will give a dollar to whoever gets the answer. Tell people they will never guess what it is that kills more drivers than anything else in America. A few more shouts emit from the crowd. People are now waiting around for the answer. What is it that kills more drivers than anything else in the United States? What is it that could be the death of you and me? You won't believe this, but it is "trees." Millions of them line our highways, waiting for a driver to kill. When one is struck, the tree stays still, sending the driver into eternity.

Then tell the crowd that you have another question for them. Ask what they think is the most common food on which people choke to death in US restaurants. Over the next few minutes, go through the same scenario. People call out "Steak!" "Chicken bones!" Believe it or not, the answer is "hard-boiled egg yolk."

By now you have a crowd that is enjoying what is going on. Ask them what they think is the most dangerous job in America. Someone calls out "cop." It's not. Someone else may name another dangerous profession like "firefighter." Say, "Good one ... but wrong." Give a suggestion by saying, "Why doesn't someone say 'electrician'?" Someone takes the suggestion and says, "Electrician!" Say, "Sorry, it's not electrician." The most dangerous job in the United States... is to be the president. Out of forty or so, four have been murdered while on the job (McKinley, Garfield, Lincoln, and Kennedy).

Then tell the crowd you have another question. "Does anyone in the crowd consider himself to be a good person?" The Bible tells us that "most men will proclaim each his own goodness" (Proverbs 20:6), and someone does. He smiles and says, "Yes, I do consider myself to be a good person." Ask him if he has ever told a lie. Has he stolen, lusted, blasphemed, etc.? That's when all Heaven breaks loose. Sinners hear the gospel, there is conviction of sin, "godly sorrow produces repentance leading to salvation" (2 Corinthians 7:10), and the angels rejoice.

Another way to draw responses is to address trivia questions to those in the crowd who embrace evolution. Simply say, "This next question is only for those who believe in evolution." Then ask these questions (giving away dollar bills for correct answers): "What was Darwin's first name?" *(Charles)* "What was the name of his first book?" *(The Voyage of the Beagle)* "What is the age of the earth: thousands, millions, or billions of years old?"

While people are calling out answers, look for the most outspoken person. Then ask him, "What's your name? Fred, you obviously believe in the theory of evolution. Why?"

Don't feel that you need to be an expert on the theory of evolution or even have to give your thoughts on the age of the earth. All you have to remember is that you are completely in control of the *direction* of the conversation and can move from the "intellect" (the place of argument) to the "conscience" (the place of the knowledge of right and wrong) anytime you wish by taking him through the moral Law. Simply ask him questions about why he believes what he believes about the theory, then ask if he believes in the existence of God—is there a Heaven, etc.? If he says that he doesn't believe in God or an afterlife, say, "*If* Heaven does exist, are you good enough to go there? Are you a good person?" This moves away from the intellect to the conscience. Then take him through the Commandments. If he says that he is not a good person, ask, "So have you broken the Ten Commandments?" and take him through each one for his (and for the crowd's) sake. Then preach Judgment Day, the cross, the resurrection, repentance, and faith.

For years our team has used a flipchart to help draw a crowd. We use this almost every time we open-air preach. Sometimes it's purely a backdrop to visually show passersby that the speaker isn't merely on a rant on top of a soapbox, but is doing an interactive presentation—giving people more confidence to pause and listen. Other times, we use each page as an illustrative tool.

The chart contains a number of fascinating intelligence questions that most people get wrong, such as, "How many of each animal did Moses take onto the ark?" Most say, "Two." Everyone

*Scotty is using both a trivia book and a flip chart at Huntington Beach.
Visuals are very helpful in getting people's attention.*

*When using the flip chart, we hang bags on the easel as weights
to stop the wind from blowing it over.*

laughs when they realize that it was Noah (not Moses) who built the ark. It has the effect of humbling the person and at the same time increasing the crowd. It's fun but it has serious results. It shows our listeners that we have a sense of humor—that we are different from angry preachers who stand on street corners yelling at people. And when someone is humbled they are more likely to listen to the gospel. We also have a trivia book that I have used hundreds of times to draw a crowd.[3]

As I mentioned earlier, over the years I've tried everything under the sun to attract a crowd. Some things work and some don't. If the previous suggestions don't appeal to you, or you've tried them and they don't work well for you, I've found that nothing gets the attention of the world like a funeral. I have done many mock funerals, where someone is lying on the ground covered with a sheet and surrounded by pallbearers. I may have "mourners" gather around as I preach. These funerals never fail

A mock funeral on Main Street, Huntington Beach, California

to draw a crowd, and they also make it easy to springboard from speaking of death into the gospel of everlasting life.

I usually say that nothing gets our attention like death. It will be the biggest day of our life because that's when we pass into eternity. Or that most have heard the saying that only two things in life are sure: death and taxes. That's not true. Plenty of people avoid taxes; nobody avoids death. Then I ask, "So how are you going to do when you die and face God? Are you a good person?"

Back in New Zealand at one of these mini-dramas, one of the female mourners was sobbing just before I was due to speak. She had gone to the local Salvation Army store and purchased black clothes, a black hat, and a black veil. I was supposed to be a sober-faced priest (I did have minister's credentials at the time), and this young lady was overdoing her part. Her sobs were so loud I could feel laughter welling up inside me, and I knew that if I didn't do something quick I was going to burst out laughing and wreck the funeral.

So I slowly walked over to her in front of the large crowd, put my comforting hand on her heaving shoulder, leaned forward and gently whispered, "Shut up." It was a funny moment.

But on a more serious note, may I encourage you to do this? All it takes is a lot of love and a little boldness. You just do it as you would a real funeral, reminding those who gather that they have an appointment to keep, and thoroughly preach the gospel as you do so.

BRIDGE BUILDING IS KEY

You may have your own open-air "Greek poets" bridge. I have mine. For the last twenty or so years I have found that simple trivia questions are an effective way to connect with passing strangers, whom I want to have stop and listen to the gospel. By asking interesting questions and giving away money for correct (and even incorrect) answers, I'm able to quietly build favor and credibility with my listeners before I share the message.

Our problem is that the prescription we advocate has an unpleasant taste in the mouth of sinners. The message, when presented biblically, is bitter medicine indeed. If we are to be faithful, we must share sin, righteousness, and judgment. The guilt of sin, the necessity of repentance, the fearful subject of sure death, the pain of a stirred conscience, and talk of the reality of Hell are hard for the world to swallow. So it's vital that they believe we have a friendly, caring demeanor.

> *"My anxious desire in that every time I preach, I may clear myself of blood of all men; that if I step from this platform to my coffin, I may have told out all I knew of the way of salvation."* —CHARLES SPURGEON

With the help of God, I want to resonate with my hearers. Even before I turn to the subject at hand, I want them to know that I'm reasonable and that I'm motivated by love and kindness. When trivia questions are asked, answers are offered, and money is given away to winners—and to people who don't deserve it because they get a wrong answer—those few moments are very important and precious. It's a small thing that provides a huge advantage when the message is shared, because it gives me their ears, and without that I may as well not preach.

CHAPTER 7

DEALING WITH HECKLERS

How would the common people have become indoctrinated with the gospel had it not been for those far-wandering evangelists... and those daring innovators who found a pulpit on every heap of stones, and an audience chamber in every open space near the abodes of men?

—CHARLES SPURGEON

As noted earlier, hecklers aren't something you should fear; they're something you should pray for. A heckler can be just the bait you're looking for as you fish for men, instantly turning a small, lackluster gathering into a large and lively crowd. Knowing how to respond to those who bully you can make all the difference. In this chapter, we'll consider how to handle any hecklers you may be blessed to have—whether they're too talkative, too quiet, angry, atheists, false converts, or more.

A VARIETY OF HECKLERS

A "good" heckler is one who will provoke your thoughts. He (or she) will stand up, speak up, and then shut up so that you can preach. Occasionally, you will get hecklers who have the first two qualifications, but they just won't be quiet. If they will not let you get a word in, as a last resort, move your location. Usually, most of the crowd will follow. It is better to have ten listeners who can hear than two hundred who can't. If the heckler follows, move again... then the crowd will usually turn on him.

One tactic that often works with a heckler who is out solely to hinder the gospel is to wait until he is quiet and say to the crowd (making sure the heckler is listening also), "I want to show you how people are like sheep. When I move, watch this man follow me because he can't get a crowd by himself." The crowd moves, but his pride usually keeps him from following.

If the heckler is reasonable (or wants to look as though he is), you can say, "Both of us yelling is confusing. How about I let you speak for two minutes, and then you let me speak for two minutes. Okay?" Once you have his okay, then hold him to it if he doesn't keep his word. Make sure you keep yours. I can usually get the gospel out in two minutes. Practice a short presentation in case you have to use it.

If you have a "mumbling heckler" who won't speak up, ignore him and talk over the top of him. This will usually get him angry enough to speak up and draw hearers. There is a fine line between him getting angry enough to draw a crowd, and hitting you; you will find it in time.

If you are fortunate enough to get a heckler, don't panic. Show him genuine respect, not only because he may double your crowd, but because the Bible says to honor all men (1 Peter

2:17), so you don't want to offend him unnecessarily. If you say something that's a little unkind, be quick to apologize. It is humbling to do so, but you will get the respect of the crowd, and you want that for the sake of them listening to what you have to say.

Always ask the heckler his name, so that if you want to ask him a question and he is talking to someone, you don't have to say, "Hey, you!" If he won't give you his name, you may like to make one up. I usually choose "Bob."

Often, people will walk through the crowd so they can get close to you and will whisper something like, "I think you are a #@*!$!" Answer loud enough for the crowd to hear, "God bless you." Do it with a smile so that it looks as though the person has just whispered a word of encouragement to you. This will stop him from doing it again. The Bible says to bless those who curse you (Luke 6:28), so ask God to bless him. Remember that you are not fighting against flesh and blood. Many times I have had hecklers spit out venom, and approach me afterward almost bewildered at how nasty they were.

Hecklers may stoop very low and be cutting and cruel in their remarks. If you have some physical disability, they will play on it. I put myself down before they can. If they ask why I'm standing on a box, I say "Because I'm short." When I do trivia, I often ask, "How tall do you think this little body is?" and give a dollar to anyone who gets it right. If they insult you, try to smile back at them. Look past the words. If you are reviled for the name of Jesus, "rejoice, and be exceeding glad." Read Matthew 5:10–12 until it is written on the corridors of your mind.

The most angry hecklers are usually what we call "backsliders." These are actually false converts who never slid forward in the first place. They "asked Jesus into their heart" but never truly repented. When someone says that he "used to be a Christian," ask him, "Did you know the Lord?" (see Hebrews 8:11). If he answers "Yes," then he is admitting that he is willfully denying Him, and if he answers "No," then he was never a Christian in the first place: "This is eternal life, that they might know you, the only true God, and Jesus Christ, whom you have sent" (John 17:3). (For more on the vital topic of false converts, see chapter 9.)

"Love your fellowmen, and cry about them if you cannot bring them to Christ. If you cannot save them, you can weep over them. If you cannot give them a drop of water in hell, you can give them your heart's tears while they are still in this body."
—CHARLES SPURGEON

THE UNCONCERNED CHRISTIAN

By far the most difficult dilemma in which you will find yourself is an encounter with a professing Christian who has no concern for the lost. This sort of person will usually burst into your crowd and say, "I'm a Christian, and you're doing this all wrong!" To know what spirit motivates them, you need only watch who sides with this person. Often, the nastiest of nasty hecklers will high-five this person. It's interesting that people who would normally be enemies will become friends and unify in their anti-Christian spirit. The Bible says that Herod and Pilate were enemies but they became friends in their stand against Jesus (Luke 23:12).

These professing Christians will accuse you of being unloving and judgmental. However, they are the ones who lack love for people because they know sinners will go to Hell if they die in their sins, but they don't bother to warn them. You will have to pray for special patience with these people, because they are usually very unreasonable, and they feel they are speaking on behalf of God when they publicly rebuke you.

So this is what I do in this difficult situation. I ask them publicly to say where the crowd will go if they die in their sins. They will usually try to get out of this so you have to hold their feet to the fire. Have them admit that people who die in their sins will not go to Heaven but will go to Hell. From there say, "Then please get up on this box and warn these people. I will sit at your feet and listen to how you do it." At this point, they normally back down and leave.

It seems that much of the modern church has forgotten about Hell. Never forget that that is the reason we preach: "Knowing, therefore, the terror of the Lord, we persuade men" (2 Corinthians 5:11). We are to warn every man that we may present every man perfect in Christ Jesus (Colossians 1:28). If Hell didn't exist, neither would my ministry. I would be a happy Christian enjoying the pleasures of this temporal life. But it does exist, and it grieves me to a point of tears that some have no tears that this world is going to Hell.

"God save us from living in comfort while sinners are sinking into Hell!" —CHARLES SPURGEON

I once read where someone said that Hell is a "hideous" doctrine, and that if God was love He would never create such a place. Then let's follow that logic and, as loving human beings, completely do away with prisons because they are hideous places.

However, that would be a hard sell with those whose daughters have been raped and murdered, or with those whose life's savings have been embezzled. Such people call for justice, not for "love." A judge may be a loving man, but he sits in court not to exhibit love but to ensure that justice is done.

For a professing Christian to say that there is no such place as Hell is to be a Judas to the cause of Christ. It is to pat a blind man on the back as he taps his way toward a thousand-foot cliff. It is love that drives us to warn every blind sinner that if they refuse to turn away from sin and trust in Jesus alone, they will fall into the hands of the living God, and the Bible says that is a "fearful thing" (Hebrews 10:31). (For more on what the Bible says about Hell, see appendix B.)

Don't be disheartened if people cut you off because of what you say about sin and judgment, or walk away from the crowd seemingly untouched. Remember that the rich young ruler walked away from Jesus because he loved his sin. So if Jesus sometimes lost His hearers (as in this case and in other places), how much more will we?

THE UNIVERSALIST

If a heckler says that everyone goes to Heaven, he's called a "universalist." Universalism is the belief that God will save everyone. It's a form of idolatry—creating a god in our own image, other than the One revealed in Holy Scripture, which says that God will by no means clear the guilty (Exodus 34:7).

When I encounter someone who believes that everyone will go to Heaven, I ask if he thinks Hitler will make it, and reason with him about what God should do to someone who merci-lessly slaughtered Jewish families—more than six million men, women, and children. Most people suddenly see the need for Hell. Then I reason with him. If a human judge doesn't do all he can to see that justice is done, he is corrupt and should be brought to justice himself. How much more will God have His Day of retribution? If He is good, He must bring about ultimate justice. If a universalist has out-of-context Scriptures to back up his wrong doctrine, quote Matthew 7:14: "Because narrow is the gate and difficult is the way which leads to life, and there are few who find it," or Matthew 25:46: "These will go away into ever-lasting punishment, but the righteous into eternal life."

Again, the root of the universalist's deception is idolatry. There's a reason that the first two of the Ten Commandments address idolatry. We have a natural bias toward it. The Bible warns, "Do not be deceived. Neither fornicators, nor idolaters, nor adulterers, nor homosexuals, nor sodomites... will inherit the kingdom of God" (1 Corinthians 6:9,10). It's important to note that "idolaters" seems to be the odd one out. Idolatry (mak-ing up a false god) may seem strange in a list of sexual sins among others.

But it's there because when we make up a false god, it doesn't tell us what is right or wrong. When we create a god in our image (whether it's an idol made of wood or stone or an image of God we imagine in our minds), that idol doesn't speak, and therefore anything becomes morally permissible—whether it's fornication, adultery, lust, or homosexuality. Idolatry opens the doorway to immorality and closes it to immortality. So every unsaved person with whom you will deal in an open-air session is an idolater. The Bible says that there is none who understands or seeks after God (Romans 3:11). With the help of God, your job is to present the majesty of God as revealed in Holy Scripture, and the most effective way to do that is through revelation of His righteousness... and you can do that through the Law.

The way to get rid of an idol is to do what Moses did when Israel had made their own image of God and danced around their golden calf. He threw the Ten Commandments at their sin-loving feet, showing them that they have broken the Law into a thousand pieces. Do the same. Take sinners through the moral Law and watch it make judgment and Hell make sense. Reason with them as Paul reasoned with Felix—about sin, righteousness, and judgment to come—and pray that they tremble as Felix did (Acts 20:24,25).

"To this day field preaching is a cross to me, but I know my commission and see no other way of preaching the gospel to every creature." —JOHN WESLEY

Charles Spurgeon said,

You are dying; many of you when you die must perish forever; it is not for me to be amusing you with some deep things that may instruct your intellect but do not enter your hearts; it is for me to fit the arrow to the string and send it home—to unsheathe the sword—be the scabbard never so glittering, to cast it aside, and let the majesty of naked truth smite at your hearts.

So never be fearful to preach words that produce fear. Fear is not always the enemy. It keeps us from stepping off cliffs or getting too close to fire, and in doing so becomes our friend. A little healthy fear and trembling, as with Felix, is the first sign of conviction. The preaching of sin, righteousness, and judgment should result in the fear of God, and "by the fear of the LORD one departs from evil" (Proverbs 16:6).

THE ATHEIST

If someone professes to be an atheist, ask, "As an atheist, do you believe the scientific impossibility that nothing created everything?" If he says that he does, emphasize that it's scientifically impossible for nothing to create everything, and leave him with that. If he doesn't believe that (which most admit they don't), follow with, "So you believe that something made everything, but it just wasn't God?"

If he says, "Yes, that's right," then tell him, "Well, you're not an atheist then. You're an agnostic. You believe in some sort of creative force but you don't think it was God. Let's see if we can find out why you don't want it to be God." If he lets you speak further, take him through the Ten Commandments and you will find out that the issue isn't intellectual, it's moral. He's a liar, a thief, a blasphemer, and an adulterer at heart who knows that God exists, but (as someone once wisely said) he can't find God for the same reason a thief can't find a policeman.[4]

Keep in mind that we do not have to prove to the atheist that God exists. He intuitively knows that God exists but willfully suppresses the truth (see Romans 1:18). Every person has a God-given conscience, which is the "work of the law written in their hearts" (Romans 2:15). Just as every sane person knows that it is wrong to lie, steal, kill, and commit adultery, he also knows that if there is a moral Law, then there must be a moral Lawgiver.

In addition to the testimony of his impartial conscience, the atheist also has the testimony of creation. It declares the glory of God, His eternal power, and divine nature, so that the person who denies the voice of conscience and the voice of creation is without excuse (Psalm 19:1; Romans 1:19–21). If he dies in his sins, he will face the wrath of a holy Creator, whether he believes in Him or not.

This is why I don't spend too much effort trying to convince anyone that there is a God. To do so is to waste time and energy. What sinners need is not to be convinced that God exists, but that their sin exists and that they are in terrible danger. The only biblical way to do this is to go through the moral Law and explain that God considers lust to be adultery and hatred to be murder, etc. It is the revelation that God is holy and just, and sees the thought-life, that convinces us that we are in danger of eternal damnation. That is what sinners need to hear to send them to the cross for mercy. So never be discouraged from preaching the gospel, and don't get sidetracked by rabbit-trail issues that don't really matter—like the foolishness of evolution.

I once said, "Forget the chicken and the egg—which came first, the air or the lungs, the heart or the blood, the male or the female, water or thirst, food or the stomach? Stop the confusion. Read Genesis." That's when a believer in Darwinian evolution stepped up to the plate and answered each question, ending with "science has evidence for its answers."

He believed that air came first. But if the air came first, where did it come from, and how was it that it had just the right amount of oxygen to sustain human life? While human lungs were evolving, how did we breathe? Why did they evolve if life was already sustained without them?

Next he believed that our incredibly complex blood formed before the heart. Why did it do that, and how did it get around the body if there was no heart to pump it?

He believed that male and female (for some reason) gradually evolved at the same time. They had to because they needed each other to survive, as did each of the millions of species, each of which have male and female. Why and how did evolution cause these millions of different species to evolve as male and female, each with different (but corresponding) reproductive parts? How did they reproduce while these parts were supposedly evolving?

Next he believed that water evolved before thirst. We know that we can't live without water, so how did we (and the millions of animals) survive if we had no thirst?

He also believed that food evolved before the stomach. So eggs, wheat, beef, cabbage, potatoes, tomatoes, apples, and a million and one other amazing foods evolved, but we couldn't eat anything because the stomach hadn't evolved? Nor had our teeth, tongue, taste buds, epiglottis, esophagus, digestive juices, or small and large intestines.

I am amazed at how such an unthinkable, unproven, and unprovable theory has survived for all these years, and that some have the gall to believe that it's even slightly scientific.

Genesis simply and plainly tells us that all creation was brought into being at once by the hand of Almighty God. And that's not a pleasant thought for sin-loving sinners.

FOCUS ON THE GOSPEL

Keep in mind the worldview of this godless and sin-denying world. If someone does something that society sees as morally wrong, the secular worldview says his actions were not because he is evil, but because of some mitigating circumstance. Perhaps he lacked a father figure, or he was bullied as a child, or he was a loner that no one understood, etc. Therefore he shouldn't be punished but instead should be rehabilitated to be a productive member of society. It is because of this brainwashing that they flinch at divine retribution. But don't let that cause you to flinch from preaching an uncompromising gospel.

We are living in an age where criminal law is no longer feared. If you wanted to collect on someone's life insurance, nowadays you could have a hit man take him out and if statistics hold true there's only a fifty-percent chance you will get caught. If you do get caught, with a good lawyer and a sympathetic jury, the odds are that you will get at most ten years in prison. There you will be given a free room with a TV, free food, and a steady job as they "rehabilitate" rather than punish you. On top of that you might get out early for good behavior. And so we had 200,000 murders in the US in just one ten-year period (1990–2000). But if we were a truly God-fearing nation, there wouldn't be any murder. There wouldn't even be hatred.

Tragically, we will see more of the same as America becomes more secularized. So expect those whose minds have been soaked in this worldview to fight anything you say about sin, righteousness, and judgment and to reject the authority of the Bible.

It's easy to understand why the world hates the Bible. If it is truly God's Word, they are accountable for their theft, fornication, homosexuality, sinful imaginations, and lust (which Scripture says is adultery of the heart). So the hill on which they will die is to prove that the God of the Bible is unjust in His judgments, and therefore any thoughts of Judgment Day and Hell are bogus. They are searching after truth about as much as a man dying of thirst searches for salt. They rather want to bolster their case for an evil God, so they fortify themselves behind what they believe are mistakes, contradictions, atrocities, etc., in the Bible's pages.

For example, what do you say if a heckler tries to discredit God by blaming Him for starving children? Is God guilty because He doesn't provide them with better nutrition? After all, He is the Creator.

The way I deal with questions about specific human suffering is to broaden the question. I try to show them things are much worse than the issue they are addressing. The horror of starving children is just one of the problems. Why doesn't God help the thousands of children who die of cancer each year or those kids who are sold into prostitution, or those who are molested by pedophiles? Why doesn't He also help the adults who are starving, those dying of disease, those being raped, tortured, and the many thousands who are murdered? Why doesn't He step in and save the 150,000 people who die every twenty-four hours through disease, accidents, tornadoes, earthquakes, hurricanes, floods, etc.?

Here is the answer for all of those issues: The Bible says that we live in a fallen creation, and that tornadoes, earthquakes, hurricanes, floods, disease, and terrible human suffering are the results of our sin. When God made Adam and Eve, the Scriptures say that everything was "very good," but when they disobeyed and sin entered the world, it brought with it endless suffering. Man is therefore to blame for death, disease, and suffering—not God.

It's also important to note that God isn't the divine butler many consider Him to be. He doesn't come running when we snap our fingers to have our problems fixed. So is He guilty of a heartless negligence? The key to finding the answer is to take the questioner through the Law, and if he answers each question with an honest heart it will stop the foolishness of standing in moral judgment over a morally perfect Creator.

Be aware that if a heckler speaks of the atrocity of slavery being advocated in the Bible, and you explain that biblical slavery was akin to being a servant to pay off debt, the skeptic will just come back with more problems he has with the Scriptures. The only effective way to deal with him is to move away from his contentious intellect (his carnal mind) and appeal to his God-given conscience by taking him through the moral Law.

> "The conscience of a man, when he is really quickened and awakened by the Holy Spirit, speaks the truth. It rings the great alarm bell. And if he turns over in his bed, that great alarm bell rings out again and again, 'The wrath to come! The wrath to come! The wrath to come.'"
>
> —CHARLES SPURGEON

With the help of God, your aim is to make him thirst after righteousness. It was only when I saw my sins (way back in 1972) that I began to see my danger and whisper, "What must I do to be made right with God?" The salt of the Law made me thirst for the righteousness that can be found only in Christ.

This is why we need to keep in mind that it's the gospel that is "the power of God to salvation" (Romans 1:16). We can easily get so caught up in apologetics that we forget to preach the cross. And it's easy to do because it is intellectually stimulating. It's important to always remember that apologetics address the intellect and don't bring conviction of sin. I have seen many open-air situations where the discussion goes on and on and degenerates into an argument.

The Bible warns us to avoid foolish questions because they start arguments (2 Timothy 2:23). Most of us have fallen into the trap of jumping at every objection to the gospel. However, these questions can often sidetrack you from the "weightier matters of the Law" (Matthew 23:23). While apologetics (arguments for God's existence, creation vs. evolution, etc.) are legitimate in evangelism, they should merely be "bait," with the Law of God being the "hook" that brings the conviction of sin. Those who witness solely in the realm of apologetical argument may just get an intellectual decision rather than a repentant conversion. The sinner may come to a point of acknowledging that the Bible is the Word of God and Jesus is Lord—but even the devil knows that.

Always pull the sinner back to his responsibility before God on Judgment Day, as Jesus did in Luke 13:1–5. Whenever you are in an open-air situation, be wary of those who are intent on distracting workers from witnessing. They argue about prophecy, how much water one should baptize with, or in whose name they should be baptized. It is grievous to see five or six Christians standing around arguing with some sectarian nitpicker, while sinners are sinking into hell.

It is the cross that a sinner needs to hear about. Paul said, "For I determined not to know anything among you except Jesus Christ and Him crucified" (1 Corinthians 2:2). In Athens, Paul used apologetics (briefly) as a highway to the cross. That was his destination. Apologetics should be a means to an end, not the end itself. So always keep that in mind, both in preaching and in personal witnessing.

When I took our team to Santa Monica we had something we would do when the person preaching on the soapbox forgot to preach the cross. It sounds strange, but it was a common occurrence. We would start with trivia and a crowd would build. Then a heckler would get upset, and the crowd would become even larger as they listened to an interesting discourse about atheism or evolution. The crowd loved it because there was no mention of "sin, righteousness, and judgment." Suddenly we would realize that thirty minutes had gone by, and nothing was being said by the preacher about the cross. So one of us would walk by and gently tap his ankle as a reminder, and he would then say, "Let's leave this subject for a moment. Do you think you are a good person?"

> *"The motto of all true servants of God must be, 'We preach Christ; and Him crucified.' A sermon without Christ in it is like a loaf of bread without any flour in it. No Christ in your sermon, sir? Then go home, and never preach again until you have something worth preaching."*
>
> —CHARLES SPURGEON

I have determined that I will never be distracted from preaching Christ crucified for the sin of the world. I hope you are the same. Paul said, "For I determined not to know anything among you except Jesus Christ and Him crucified" (1 Corinthians 2:2).

RECOMMENDED VIDEOS

Go to LivingWaters.com/OAP to watch the following clips:

HECKLER'S BOX & CHALK LINE: Huntington Beach Open-Air #21

UNREASONABLE HECKLER: Crowd Turns Against Preacher

OBNOXIOUS HECKLER: Huntington Beach Open-Air #10

BRINGING HECKLERS BACK TO JUDGMENT DAY: Huntington Beach Open-Air #2

CHAPTER 8

THE IMPORTANCE OF THE RESPONSE

*Sin and hell are married unless repentance
proclaims the divorce.*

—CHARLES SPURGEON

Joseph Parker (English preacher, 1830–1902) said, "The man whose little sermon is 'repent' sets himself against his age, and will for the time being be battered mercilessly by the age whose moral tone he challenges. There is but one end for such a man: 'off with his head!' You had better not try to preach until you have pledged your head to heaven."

It's not what most modern preachers say that bothers me; it's what they don't say. They often don't talk about sin, or that God requires perfect righteousness, or the reality of Hell's existence. And so they rarely preach Christ crucified to save sinners from God's wrath, when that should be the very heart and soul of the gospel message.

As you witness, divorce yourself from the thought that you are merely seeking "decisions for Christ." What we should be seeking is repentance within the heart. This is the purpose of the Law, to bring the knowledge of sin. How can a man repent if he doesn't know what sin is? If there is no repentance, there is no salvation. Jesus said, "Unless you repent you will all likewise perish" (Luke 13:3). God is not willing that any should perish, but that all should come to repentance (2 Peter 3:9).

"A foolish physician he is, and a most unfaithful friend, that will let a sick man die for fear of troubling him; and cruel wretches are we to our friends, that will rather suffer them to go quietly to hell, then we will anger them, or hazard our reputation with them." —RICHARD BAXTER

Many don't understand that the salvation of a soul is not a resolution to change a way of life, but *"repentance toward God and faith toward our Lord Jesus Christ"* (Acts 20:21, emphasis added). The modern concept of success in evangelism is to relate how many people were "saved" (that is, how many prayed the "sinner's prayer"). This produces a "no decisions, no success" mentality. This shouldn't be, because Christians who seek decisions in evangelism become discouraged after a time of witnessing if "no one came to the Lord." The Bible tells us that as we sow the good seed of the gospel, one sows and another reaps (John 4:37). If you faithfully sow the seed, someone will reap. If you reap, it is because someone has sown in the past, but it is God who causes the seed to grow. If His hand is not on the person you are leading in a prayer of committal, if there is no God-given repentance, then you will end up with a stillbirth on your hands, and that is nothing to rejoice about. We should measure our success by how faithfully we sowed the seed. In that way, we will avoid becoming discouraged.

LORDSHIP SALVATION

There is contention among some Christians because I preach repentance and faith and so they accuse me of preaching what they call "Lordship salvation." One particular gentleman called me a wolf and a false prophet for teaching "damnable heresy."

I would like to address this because the issue of repentance is a hill on which to die. Some maintain that sinners are saved by faith in Jesus alone. Once they are saved, they then are to repent. So to tell sinners to repent or to forsake their sins is considered "works" salvation and is therefore heretical.

The foundational truth of salvation is that we are saved by grace and grace alone: "For by grace you have been saved through faith, and that not of yourselves; it is the gift of God, not of works, lest anyone should boast" (Ephesians 2:8,9).

We're not are saved *by* faith but rather *through* faith. Faith is the means by which we receive the amazing grace that saves us. Those who wrongly believe that faith alone saves us call repentance a "work," and at the same time require that a sinner must have faith to be saved...that all he must "do" is believe in Jesus. Even the demons believe (James 2:19), yet they are not saved. Scripture is clear that sinners must also repent:

- The first public word Jesus preached was "repent" (Matthew 4:17).

- John the Baptist began his ministry the same way (Matthew 3:2).

- Jesus called sinners to repent: "I have not come to call the righteous, but sinners, to repentance" (Luke 5:32).

- Jesus commanded that we preach repentance: "that repentance and remission of sins should be preached in His name to all nations…" (Luke 24:47).

- The disciples obeyed the command to call sinners to repentance: "So they went out and preached that people should repent" (Mark 6:12).

- The Bible also speaks of "repentance to salvation" (2 Corinthians 7:10) as well as "repentance to life" (Acts 11:18).

NOTE THE ORDER

Sinners are to both repent and believe. Jesus preached, "Repent, and believe in the gospel" (Mark 1:15). The apostle Paul preached "repentance toward God and faith toward our Lord Jesus Christ" (Acts 20:21). Note that the order of repentance in both of these cases is *before* faith.

Preaching on the Day of Pentecost, Peter commanded his hearers to repent: "Repent, and let every one of you be baptized in the name of Jesus Christ for the remission of sins; and you shall receive the gift of the Holy Spirit" (Acts 2:38). Notice the call to repentance before the receiving of the gift. Without repentance, there is no remission of sins. Peter further said, "Repent therefore and be converted, that your sins may be blotted out" (Acts 3:19). We cannot be "converted" unless we repent.

Paul likewise told his unsaved hearers to repent: "Truly, these times of ignorance God overlooked, but now commands all men everywhere to repent…" (Acts 17:30). All men, without exception, must repent.

James called sinners to repentance: "Cleanse your hands, you sinners; and purify your hearts, you double-minded. Lament and mourn and weep! Let your laughter be turned to mourning and your joy to gloom" (James 4:8).

The unsaved must be genuinely sorry for their sins because "godly sorrow produces repentance leading to salvation" (2 Corinthians 7:10). Repentance leads to salvation.

GOD IS WAITING FOR SINNERS TO REPENT

The Scriptures tell us that God isn't willing that any perish, but is patiently waiting for all to come to repentance:

> The Lord is not slack concerning His promise, as some count slackness, but is longsuffering toward us, not willing that any should perish but that all should come to repentance. (2 Peter 3:9)

Without repentance, sinners will perish. Look at the fate of those who refused to repent:

> But the rest of mankind, who were not killed by these plagues, did not repent of the works of their hands, that they should not worship demons, and idols of gold, silver, brass, stone, and wood, which can neither see nor hear nor walk. And they did not repent of their murders or their sorceries or their sexual immorality or their thefts. (Revelation 9:20,21)

The Scriptures say, "He who covers his sins will not prosper, but whoever confesses and forsakes them will have mercy" (Proverbs 28:13). Mercy comes when we confess and forsake our sins (repent). Jesus tells us that Heaven rejoices when a sinner obeys the command to repent: "There is joy in the presence of the angels of God over one sinner who repents" (Luke 15:10). If there is no repentance, there is no joy because there is no salvation.

General William Booth warned that the time would come when forgiveness would be offered without repentance:

> The chief danger of the 20th century will be . . . forgiveness without repentance, salvation without regeneration, politics without God, and Heaven without Hell.

John Wesley believed that there is no justification without repentance:

> God does undoubtedly command us both to repent, and to bring forth fruits meet for repentance; which if we willingly neglect, we cannot reasonably expect to be justified at all: therefore both repentance, and fruits meet for repentance, are, in some sense, necessary to justification.[5]

Matthew Henry said, "If those who have lived a wicked life repent and forsake their wicked ways, they shall be saved . . ."

A. W. Pink wrote in *Studies on Saving Faith:*

> Something more than "believing" is necessary to salvation. A heart that is steeled in rebellion against God cannot savingly believe: it must first be broken. It is written "except ye repent, ye shall all likewise perish" (Luke 13:3). Repentance is just as essential as faith, yea, the latter cannot be without the former: "Repented not afterward, that ye might believe" (Matt. 21:32).

Spurgeon added, "Offend or please, as God shall help me, I will preach every truth as I learn it from the Word; and I know if there be anything written in the Bible at all it is written as with a sunbeam, that God in Christ commands men to repent, and believe the gospel."

Another argument some give for not preaching repentance is that the Gospel of John doesn't even mention the word "repentance" once. But neither do any of the other three Gospels mention the need to be born again, nor do Mark or John mention the virgin birth.

WHAT IS REPENTANCE?

One catalyst for the teaching that repentance is unnecessary for salvation is the belief that repentance is merely "a change of mind." This erroneous teaching is nothing new. Spurgeon had to deal with it in his day:

> Apparently they interpret repentance to be a somewhat slighter thing than we usually conceive it to be, a mere change of mind, in fact. Now, allow me to suggest to those dear brethren, that the Holy Ghost never preaches repentance as a trifle; and the change of mind or understanding of which the gospel speaks is a very deep and solemn work, and must not on any account be depreciated . . . There must be sorrow for sin and hatred of it in true repentance, or else I have read my Bible to little purpose.[6]

The Scriptures say, "Let the wicked *forsake his way*, and the unrighteous man his thoughts" (Isaiah 55:7, emphasis added). Repentance is a turning away from sin:

"Repent, *turn away* from your idols, and *turn your faces away* from all your abominations." (Ezekiel 14:6)

"But if a wicked man *turns from all his sins* which he has committed, keeps all My statutes, and does what is lawful and right, he shall surely live; he shall not die." (Ezekiel 18:21)

"To you first, God, having raised up His Servant Jesus, sent Him to bless you, in *turning away every one of you from your iniquities.*" (Acts 3:26)

Those in Luke 13:27 whom Jesus said He never knew were "workers of iniquity." They professed faith in Jesus but continued to serve sin. Our churches are filled with workers of iniquity (hypocrites) who were told that they merely have to believe in Jesus. For most, there's never any repentance because they have been given assurance that they are saved without it.

On Judgment Day they will understand the sobering words of Jesus when He said, "Unless you repent you will all likewise perish" (Luke 13:3).

"Those preachers who tell sinners that they may be saved without forsaking their idols, without repenting, without surrendering to the Lordship of Christ, are as erroneous and dangerous as others who insist that salvation is by works, and that heaven must be earned by our own efforts!"

—A. W. PINK

CHAPTER 9

OTHER RELIGIONS

> *As the fisherman longs to take the fish in his net,*
> *as the hunter pants to bear home his spoil, as the*
> *mother pines to clasp her lost child to her bosom,*
> *so do we faint for the salvation of souls.*
>
> —CHARLES SPURGEON

Though the gospel message we share is universal (as discussed in chapter 4), people in other religious groups have unique perceptions of how to be saved. You don't need to be an expert in the various beliefs of their religions, however; when open-air preaching, the following tips will help you quickly get to the heart of their spiritual needs.

SPEAKING WITH A JEHOVAH'S WITNESS

If you aren't sure how to share the gospel with Jehovah's Witnesses (JWs), let me tell you what I do. I say, "There's a knife in my back. I have three minutes to live. How can I enter the Kingdom?"

The biblical answer is simply to repent and trust in Jesus alone—that everlasting life is the gift of God (Ephesians 2:8,9). But JWs are a "works righteousness" religion (as are all religions outside of biblical Christianity). They think that they have to do something to earn their way into the Kingdom. They believe this because, like most religious people, they haven't seen their sin in its true light. For that, they need the moral Law, the Ten Commandments.

Think of the thief on the cross. He said that he was justly being crucified. I don't think he was saying that Roman law's capital punishment for theft was fair and just. I think he was pointing to God's Law rather than man's law. He was justly dying because he had sinned against a holy God.

It was in that hopeless condition that he turned to Jesus and said, "Lord, remember me when You come into Your kingdom" (Luke 23:42). He couldn't *do* anything because his hands were nailed to the cross. He couldn't go anywhere, because his feet were nailed to the cross.

Neither can we do anything or go anywhere to be saved, because we too have been nailed by the Law of God as guilty, deserving death and Hell. All we can do is turn to Jesus and trust in the mercy of God. We in essence say, "Lord, remember me!" And He will.

SPEAKING WITH A MUSLIM

Every Muslim's desire is to make it to Heaven and (understandably) avoid the damnation of Hell. To try to achieve salvation they fast, pray, and do religious and other good works. In that respect, a Muslim is no different than the average unsaved church-goer who hopes that God will allow him into Heaven because of his good works. And of course, we want to see both Muslims and churchgoers make it to Heaven. So how do we talk to a Muslim without making it seem as though we are proudly saying that he is wrong and we are right? I have a few thoughts.

What I'm going to say may initially sound almost heretical, but it's not. It is using discretion. If I want to awaken someone who is sleeping soundly in a dark room, I wouldn't shine a flashlight in his eyes. That would be offensive. Instead, I would use a discreet light-dimmer. We can gently relate essential biblical truths in a way that doesn't compromise but upholds Scripture. We can give light without offense.

Here goes: 1) I don't tell Muslims that Jesus is God. 2) I don't say that Jesus died "on the cross" or that He is the "Son of God," and 3) I don't say, "The Bible says..." Jesus said it's the work of the Father to reveal that Jesus is the Christ, the Son of the living God (Matthew 16:16,17). So let God handle that one. Muslims think it's blasphemous to say that God had a Son, and so it's wise to set aside certain truths until an appropriate time, if we want hearers.

Once the conversation has begun, ask him this important question: "If a man has committed very serious crimes (such as rape and murder), and he says that he is sorry and that he won't do it again, will the judge let him go?" You want him to understand that no good judge will ever dismiss such a case. He would probably be indignant, and say, "Of course the criminal should be sorry, and of course he should not do it again."

Belabor this point, because you are going to come back to it. Have him repeat his answer—that no good judge will dismiss a case just because the criminal says he is sorry and won't do it again. Help him to see that such a thought is morally ridiculous.

Now take him through the moral Law, the Ten Commandments. Show him that his Creator desires truth in the inward parts—that God sees his thought-life, and He views lust as adultery (it is wise and biblical to refer to "the prophet Jesus" when you quote Matthew 5:27,28) and hatred as murder.[7] You are aiming, with God's help, to shut him up under the Law—to leave him without excuse. You want to put him up the river Niagara without a paddle, so he will see that his salvation has to come from outside of his own futile efforts. Pray that the Holy Spirit convicts him that his sin is very serious in the eyes of a holy God.

"Brethren, do something; do something, do something! While societies and unions make constitutions, let us win souls. I pray you, be men of action all of you. Get to work and quit yourselves like men. Forward and strike! No theory! Attack! Form a column! Plunge into the center of the enemy! Our one aim is to win souls; and this we are not to talk about, but do in the power of God!"
—CHARLES SPURGEON

Then ask him if he will be innocent or guilty on Judgment Day. Will he go to Heaven or Hell? He will almost certainly say that he will make it to Heaven because he is repentant for his sin. In essence, he is telling the Judge that he is sorry and that he won't do it again.

He reveals that he is trusting in his religious works for his eternal salvation. That's when you remind him that a good judge would never dismiss a case on those grounds, and neither will God—not in a million years. God is a Judge, and we are criminals in His eyes. So anything we offer Him is an attempt to bribe Him, and the Bible says He will not be bribed. Justice must be done, and that's why he needs Someone who can wash away his sins. He needs Someone to pay his fine. That's when you tell him that God provided a Savior! The gospel is good news indeed for a humbled works-righteous Muslim.

Again, remember to belabor your illustration—that being sorry and not committing the crime again are not sufficient grounds to dismiss a case. If you don't drive that point home, you will regret it when he tries to cling to works as his hope of salvation.

SPEAKING WITH A ROMAN CATHOLIC

Most Catholics (like most non-Catholics) may go to church and be familiar with the gospel, but many lack something vital when it comes to their eternal salvation.

Let's say I meet Fred. After some friendly small talk I ask what he thinks happens after someone dies. He tells me that they go to Heaven, and then he says something I ignore. He says, "I'm Catholic." I'm deaf to that because I don't want to get into an argument about papal infallibility, Mariology, the mass, the confessional, purgatory, transubstantiation, and a number of other unbiblical doctrines. They are time-wasting rabbit trails that I choose not to go down. I'm not interested in arguing with Fred and making an enemy. I want to befriend him.

I ask Fred if he's born again. He says that he was baptized as a baby, and so I explain that the new birth is something different, that Jesus said if someone isn't born again he won't enter Heaven (see John 3), and that I want to be sure he makes it there. I bring in a serious thought by saying the difference between being born again and just believing in God is like the difference between someone just believing in a parachute and actually putting it on. The difference will be seen when they jump.

Although Fred is a committed Catholic, he has a big problem. He thinks he can make it to Heaven by being good, by believing in God, by going to mass, and by confessing his sins to a priest. With the help of God, I want to show him that the leap he's trying to make to Heaven is wider than the widest part of the Grand Canyon. My hope is that he will reconsider his beliefs before he makes the jump. So, ignoring what I've heard about him being a Catholic, I address him with the same love and concern I would anyone else who is trusting in his own righteousness, and I take him through the moral Law.

SPEAKING WITH A FALSE CONVERT

It's vital to understand the biblical teaching of true and false conversion. Without this knowledge you will be confused when "backsliders" or professing Christians try to discourage you from preaching, or when a beer-drinking, profanity-laden, fornicating blasphemer claims to be right with God because he "asked Jesus into his heart" as a child.

Someone once wrote and said, "Christ makes it clear there are three stages of being a Christian: hot, cold, and lukewarm. For being lukewarm you get spewed out of the mouth..." Let's look at what Jesus actually said, speaking to the Laodiceans:

"I know your works, that you are neither cold nor hot. I could wish you were cold or hot. So then, because you are lukewarm, and neither cold nor hot, I will vomit you out of My mouth." (Revelation 3:15,16)

There aren't "three stages of being a Christian." The Christian is either hot or cold. These are not negative attributes. A drink can be either hot and stimulating or cold and refreshing. The word "because" in reference to those who are lukewarm is the clue as to which one is the negative of the three categories.

"To offer a sinner the gift of salvation based upon the work of Christ, while at the same time allowing him to retain the idea that the gift carries with it no moral implications, is to do him untold injury where it hurts him worst."

—A. W. TOZER

The lukewarm aren't part of the Body of Christ. They merely weigh heavy within the stomach of the Body until such a time as He spews them out of His mouth. They haven't been broken down to be absorbed into the Body of Christ, to become His hands, His feet, and His mouth. Their hands don't reach out to the lost and pull sinners from the fire. Their feet aren't shod with the preparation of the gospel of peace, and their mouths don't preach the gospel to every creature.

They are filled with their own ways rather than the ways of God as they sit among God's people. They are the goats among the sheep, the tares among the wheat, the bad fish among the good, and the foolish virgins among the wise. They are the ones the Bible calls "workers of iniquity" (Luke 13:27). Those who call Jesus "Lord" and refuse to do the things that He tells them are the ones to whom He will say, "I *never* knew you; depart from Me, you who practice lawlessness!" (Matthew 7:21–23, emphasis added). They are the hypocrites, the pretenders, those who never knew the Lord (like Judas, whom Jesus referred to as a "devil"; see John 6:70). So don't be surprised when professing Christians try to stop your preaching. Attack from the enemy can be very subtle.

For more on this topic, you can listen to a free vital message, "True and False Conversion," on LivingWaters.com (at the bottom of the page). This knowledge will help you to know what's going on when someone says, "I'm a Christian and I think it's great what you are doing, but do you think you are doing any good? I think you are turning people away from God. Jesus would never do something like this," etc.

RECOMMENDED VIDEO

Go to LivingWaters.com/WOTS to watch the following clip:

PREACHING IN GUATEMALA: Entire Crowd Laughs at Him

CHAPTER 10

THE BIG
BATTLE

*The reason why many fail in battle is because
they wait until the hour of battle. The reason
why others succeed is because they have gained
their victory on their knees long before the battle
came... Anticipate your battles; fight them on
your knees before temptation comes, and you
will always have victory.*

—R. A. TORREY

B ecause you want to be on the front-line of battle, you are
going to be the target of the enemy, and one major weapon
he will use is the formidable weapon of your own lusts. Guard
your heart with all diligence. If the enemy can't take you from
without, he will take you from within.

God may have created the moth as a warning about sexual
sin. The thoughtless little creature doesn't seem to feel the heat
of the flame, nor does it see the graveyard at the base of the can-

dle. And it seems that some Christians don't feel the burning of their conscience or see the graveyard of fallen ministers who have been taken down and badly burned by sexual sin, dangerously drawn to the flames by their ungodly desires. The Bible says to flee youthful lusts (2 Timothy 2:22). If this is a particular problem you face, then preaching on a beach to nearly naked women is not the right venue for you. Be smart; pick another location. Take a leaf out of Joseph's book because Potiphar's wife is waiting for you around every corner.

It's a little embarrassing to say it, but in the beginning there was one naked couple who were told by their Maker to have sex. But then sin entered the happy scene and with it came lust and death. The "sin-lust-death" trio can never be separated, as James warns us:

> But each one is tempted when he is drawn away by his own desires and enticed. Then, when desire has conceived, it gives birth to sin; and sin, when it is full-grown, brings forth death. (James 1:14,15)

Lust always brings forth sin, and sin when it is finished always brings forth death. That's why the Bible warns us again and again about sexual sin, from Potiphar's sex-crazed wife chasing Joseph around the house, to Solomon's warning about lusty ladies, to David not being able to keep his greedy and grubby hands off another man's wife.

The Bible also tells us that these instances are written for our learning (see Romans 15:4). David was married and could have sipped from his own cistern, but he didn't because lust is blind to common sense. Instead of being in the heat of battle he was wandering the housetops burning with unlawful sexual desire. And all this was written down in Scripture for us to learn hard lessons. It's written to teach us not to have eyes full of adultery or to drink in iniquity like water because sin will have eternal repercussions.

A popular way to fight the battle is to stand arm-in-arm with other soldiers—to have accountability partners. However, this has left many a soldier mortally wounded because if someone feels okay about secretly looking at pornography (that is, he doesn't consider committing adultery in his heart as a serious sin), he will probably not see lying to his accountability partner as a serious sin either. There is an armor-plate that can solve this problem, however. It is the fear of the Lord.

If you are a man and you want to reach out to the lost, you can be sure there is a lusty lady out there with your name on her luscious lips. Lust is like a pushy, pesky, and persistent salesman who wants a foot in the door. Don't open it. Guard your heart with all diligence and put a lock on it with a healthy dose of the fear of God. Fear the One who has power to kill our body and cast our soul into Hell (Luke 12:5).

> "If any man's life at home is unworthy, he should go several miles away before he stands up to preach. When he stands up, he should say nothing." —CHARLES SPURGEON

CULTIVATE THE FEAR OF GOD

To "cultivate" the fear of the Lord means to obtain and maintain a right understanding of His burning holiness, to a point of trembling. God is absolute moral perfection. His holy eyes are in every place beholding the evil and the good (Proverbs 15:3). He will bring everything into judgment, including every secret thing whether it is good or it is evil (Ecclesiastes 12:14). All things lie naked and open to the eyes of Him to whom we have to give an account, and that includes our thought-life and our sexual imaginations (Hebrews 4:13). He destroyed Noah's generation because their imagination was continually evil. Such thoughts should help to guard our thoughts and put the fear of God in us so that when Mrs. Potiphar suddenly appears, we will say with Joseph, "How then can I do this great wickedness, and sin against God?" (Genesis 39:9).

One great key I have found in overcoming the temptation to lust is to pray for wisdom every time I am tempted. If you have the wisdom of God you will never say anything wrong or do anything wrong. God loves wisdom and the Scriptures say He will give it liberally to anyone who asks Him (James 1:5). He who gets wisdom loves his own soul. So turn the tables on temptation. Let the temptation to lust become an alarm clock to waken you to fervent prayer, and get victory over something that so often overcomes so many. *Did you get a grip on what I just said?* Don't let this slip. It works. Make temptation a loud alarm to stir you to fervently pray for wisdom. In this way, lust will cause you to seek God. This principle turns a horrible negative into a wonderful positive. It throws the hand grenade back into the face of the enemy. Determine to do this. It really works.

A pastor was once seen pacing as he was preparing to deliver his sermon. When he was asked by members of his congregation if he was nervous, he answered, "Always. But it's not you. It's Him."

Those who fear God show themselves to be true and faithful witnesses. They preach the fear of the Lord because they live in the fear of the Lord, something the Bible calls "the beginning of wisdom" (Proverbs 9:10). They are forever mindful of the presence of the Lord. We need more men and women who tremble when they preach the gospel, and may their fear of God be contagious.

SHOULD A WOMAN TESTIFY IN THE OPEN AIR?

Perhaps you would like to preach open air, but you are a woman. The moment you let your desire be known, get ready for your own battle of sorts. Someone will tell you that it's not a woman's place to preach. So let me give you my thoughts on the subject. I think the Scriptures are very clear about the place of women within the church. Women holding a place of leadership (of authority over men) within the church is unbiblical. However, I don't see any biblical grounds for the Great Commission being restricted to the male gender.

Some believe that a woman should never testify in the open air, because she would be in direct violation of Scripture: "Let a woman learn in silence with all submission. And I do not permit a woman to teach or to have authority over a man, but to be in silence" (1 Timothy 2:11,12). However, it is clear from the words "Let a woman learn in silence" that this is a reference to church conduct, not to reaching out to the lost. Paul is merely reaffirming church structure that had already been put in place within the local church:

> Let your women keep silent *in the churches*, for they are not permitted to speak; but they are to be submissive, as the law also says. And if they want to learn something, let them ask their own husbands at home; for it is shameful for women to speak *in church*. (1 Corinthians 14:34,35, emphasis added)

If Paul was speaking of the task of evangelism when he said that a woman should be silent, then all Christian women should ignore Jesus' command to "go into all the world and preach the gospel to every creature" (Mark 16:15). Instead, they should be silent. Again, if this is a general conduct admonition to the Christian woman, she should not testify either one to one or one to a hundred. She should keep silent.

However, there is no reason to believe that the Great Commission was restricted to men. God saw fit to give women the power to be witnesses on the Day of Pentecost (see Acts 1:14; 2:1–4). God had promised that this power to witness would be given to women as well as men: "And on My menservants *and on My maidservants* I will pour out My Spirit in those days" (Acts 2:18, emphasis added). When Jesus said to pray for laborers, I don't think he meant men only, and most within the Body of Christ would agree with me that every Christian, male and female, is commanded to preach the gospel to every creature.

The Bible doesn't say, "How beautiful are the feet of the men who preach the gospel of peace . . ." (Romans 10:15) or "Go [men] into all the world and preach the gospel to every creature" (Mark 16:15). In both cases the word "preach" is the Greek word *kerysso*, which means "to herald (as a public crier)." Whether you are a man or a woman, you are commanded to preach the gospel—to raise your voice as a town crier.

After the woman at the well met the Savior, she witnessed to the men in her city (see John 4:28). Did she do this on a one-to-one basis, and become silent if more than one man gathered in the open air to listen to her testify? Thank God that she wasn't silent: "And many of the Samaritans of that city believed in Him because of the word of the woman who testified, 'He told me all that I ever did'" (John 4:39).

When giving the do's and don'ts of preaching in the open air, R. A. Torrey stated, "None but consecrated men and women will ever succeed in open-air meetings." The Salvation Army, which was famous for their open-air preaching, gave women equal responsibility with men for preaching and welfare work and on one occasion cofounder William Booth remarked, "My best men are women!"

> *"Young men and old men, and sisters of all ages, if you love the Lord, get a passion for souls. Do you not see them? They are going down to hell by the thousands."*
> —CHARLES SPURGEON

The apostle Paul certainly involved women in the task of evangelism. He said, "And I urge you also, true companion, help these women who labored with me in the gospel, with Clement also, and the rest of my fellow workers, whose names are in the Book of Life" (Philippians 4:3). Women "labored" with him "in the gospel."

Scripture names a number of women who were Paul's "fellow workers" (*sunergos*) in the gospel (see Romans 16:3,9,12). This is a reference to the task of evangelism—as "those who helped [Paul] in spreading the gospel." Paul used this term not only for men but also for women, as in the case of Priscilla (Romans 16:3) and Euodia and Syntyche (Philippians 4:2). Other women Paul commends for their "labor in the Lord" were Mary, Persis, Tryphena, and Tryphosa (see Romans 16:6,12).

Charles Spurgeon included women when he spoke of Jesus making His hearers "fishers of men." Although it's not clear if he is speaking of testifying in the open air, he exhorted both men and women to evangelize:

> Now, if never before, every glow-worm must show its spark. You with the tiniest farthing candle must take it from under the bushel, and set it on a candlestick...You men and women that sit before me, you are by the shore of a great sea of human life swarming with the souls of men. You live in the midst of millions; but if you will follow Jesus, and be faithful to him, and true to him, and do what he bids you, he will make you fishers of men.

I thank God that He chose women rather than men to be first to herald the good news of the resurrected Savior. These faithful women took the good news to a group of hard-hearted,

Anna Jackson shares the gospel with a willing listener at Huntington Beach, California.

faithless men who were cringing in fear behind locked doors. That makes me wonder if the men who want women to be in silence preach in the open air themselves. Could it be that they are embarrassed by the fact that women are doing what they themselves don't have the courage to do?

God isn't averse to using women. He used Deborah as a prophet, a judge, and a deliverer in Israel (see Judges 4:4–10). What specifically is the objection to Him using women in the New Testament age, outside of the defined order of the local church? Is it because more than two people are listening to her, or because she lifts the volume of her voice? Then just think of open-air preaching as one-to-one witnessing, with some extra listeners and a little more volume. I was overjoyed when a friend sent me a video of his wife surrounded by about eighty Boy Scouts in a public park, listening to her every word—as she lovingly lifted up her voice to tell them how to find everlasting life. How could any Christian object to such a wonderful sight? But if you do still object on the grounds of your interpretation of Scripture, then read Philippians 1:15–18 and put it into practice. Rejoice with me anyway that the gospel is being preached.

When a slow car enters a freeway I have to remind myself to have grace toward the driver because his perception of speed is different from mine. The cars on the freeway seem to him to be going at a maddening pace, and it takes a minute or two of driving to adjust to the perceived faster speed.

The Scriptures tell us to have "grace" toward each other. This is because we all see things from a different perspective (I'm sure you would agree with that). What seems the right perspective on some issues to one person can seem like crazy thoughts to another, and from there contention can arise.

I thank God that there are women nowadays who love God and sinners enough to stand up and lift up their voice like a trumpet and preach the gospel to this dying world. So if you are of the female gender, ignore any discouragement. Don't hold back from reaching out to the lost in any way you can, whether it be one to one or one to a hundred.

"Many do not recognize the fact as they ought, that Satan has got men fast asleep in sin and that it is his great device to keep them so . . . We may sing songs about the sweet by and by, preach sermons and say prayers until doomsday, and he will never concern himself about us, if we don't wake anybody up. But if we awake the sleeping sinner he will gnash on us with his teeth. This is our work—to wake people up." —CATHERINE BOOTH

CHAPTER 11

GETTING CARRIED AWAY

While men go to prison, in and out, in and out,
as they do now, I'll fight; while there is a drunk-
ard left, while there is a poor lost girl upon the
streets, while there remains one dark soul
without the light of God, I'll fight—
I'll fight to the very end!

—CHARLES SPURGEON

E arly in 2015 in Huntington Beach, a young man named
Nick said he was a Christian but that he'd never been born
again. I explained that the difference between believing in God
and being born again was like the difference between believing
in a parachute and actually putting one on . . . that the difference
would be seen when he jumped.

He was listening intently as I pleaded with him to get right
with God. I said, "Nick, there are two things you need to do to

be saved. You need to repent and to trust in Jesus alone. When are you going to do that?"

At that very moment a large gentleman stepped out of the crowd, picked Nick up, and carried him away from me. I grabbed a copy of my booklet "Save Yourself Some Pain" and ran after them. The big guy had put Nick down, so I gave Nick the booklet, turned to the big guy (he must have been 6'2" and over two hundred pounds), pointed my little finger at him and said, "If I was bigger I would punch you out for what you just did. It was a big joke to you [you can see in the picture his girlfriend laughing at what he was doing], but I am deadly serious. I was talking to him about his eternal salvation, and there's nothing more important."

A stranger physically picked up my listener and carried him away at Huntington Beach, California. It was very strange.

It was at this point of time that my brain started working, and I said to myself, *What are you doing? This guy could swat you like a fly!* and went back to the crowd.

Nick told me later that he didn't even know that man, and that he really appreciated what I had said to him. I told him not to get so carried away next time, and to get right with God and read the booklet I gave him.

The following week a similar thing happened. As I was sharing the necessity of repentance and faith in Jesus with a young man, a blonde woman grabbed him by his hand and tried to pull him away. When he resisted, she pointed her finger at me and angrily hollered not to listen to me. We need to continually remind ourselves that we wrestle not against flesh and blood.

An angry woman abuses me after trying to pull away a man listening to the gospel at Huntington Beach.

There may also be occasions when a non-Christian appears to be "helping" you, like the demon-possessed woman who followed the apostle Paul:

> Now it happened, as we went to prayer, that a certain slave girl possessed with a spirit of divination met us, who brought her masters much profit by fortune-telling. This girl followed Paul and us, and cried out, saying, "These men are the servants of the Most High God, who proclaim to us the way of salvation." And this she did for many days.
>
> But Paul, greatly annoyed, turned and said to the spirit, "I command you in the name of Jesus Christ to come out of her." And he came out that very hour. (Acts 16:16–18)

The woman (or the demon) was speaking the truth. These men were servants of the Most High God, and they were showing the way of salvation. Why then was Paul grieved? Satan is very subtle. Rather than openly oppose the truth, he will often attempt to conceal it by implying that the occult and God are compatible. If you are open-air preaching, don't be surprised to have someone who is obviously demonically controlled loudly agree with you, so that it looks to the crowd that you are both preaching the same message. This is very frustrating.

For two years I was heckled almost daily by a woman named Petra. She dressed in black, carried a wooden staff, and said she was a prophet to the nation. As in the days of Noah, only eight would be saved. She maintained that she was one of them, and that she determined who the other seven would be. She also claimed that my spirit visited her spirit in the night (it did not!). The problem was that she would "Amen" much of what I preached, adding her thoughts at the points I made. She would do this at the top of her very loud voice. It must have appeared to newcomers to the crowd that we were a team, preaching the same thing. This was why I was delighted when (every now and then) she would get angry with something I said and let out a string of cuss words, revealing to the crowd that we were *not* on the same side.

When you're preaching the gospel, don't let angry reactions from your listeners concern you. A dentist knows where to work on a patient when he touches a raw nerve. When you touch a raw nerve in the heart of the sinner, it means that you are in business. Anger is a thousand times better than apathy. Anger is a sign of conviction.

Read Acts chapter 19 and see how Paul was a dentist with an eye for decay. He probed raw nerves wherever he went. At one point, he had to be carried shoulder height by soldiers because of the "violence of the mob" (Acts 21:35). Now that is a successful preacher! He didn't seek the praise of men. John Wesley said regarding his evangelist trainees, "If the gospel is preached well, sinners should be angry or convicted of sin, righteousness, and judgment to come. If they are not, then I don't think they are to be an evangelist." No doubt, he wasn't speaking about the "Jesus loves you" gospel, but about sin, Law, righteousness, judgment, and Hell.

Always follow the wisdom of Solomon: "A soft answer turns away wrath, but a harsh word stirs up anger" (Proverbs 15:1). This verse needs to be written on the hearts of all who preach the gospel, whether they share their faith with sinners one on one or preach open-air. If sinners become angry when you witness to them, speak softly. If you think you are about to be hit, ask the person his name to help diffuse the situation. Don't be afraid to gently change the subject, and don't wait to be a martyr. Jesus said to flee from a city that persecutes you (Matthew 10:23). Paul left one city in a basket (2 Corinthians 11:33).

We must never forget that we have an enemy who came "to steal, and to kill, and to destroy" (John 10:10). Jesus called him "the father of lies," and one of the greatest lies he can tell you is that you can't open your mouth for the kingdom of God. Don't believe him. With God's help you can…you can do all things through Christ who strengthens you (Philippians 4:13).

So lay aside your feelings, your fears, and your excuses. You'll be forever glad you did, because there is no greater honor on this earth than to preach the everlasting, glorious gospel of peace. Do that, and even your lowly feet will be beautiful.

> "Wesley was a preacher of righteousness. He would exalt the holiness of God, the law of God, the justice of God, the wisdom of God, the wisdom of His requirements, and the justice of His wrath. Then he would turn to the sinners and tell them of the enormity of their crimes, their open rebellion, their treason, and their anarchy." —PARIS REIDHEAD

REACHING THE UNREACHED

I would like to see more Christians reach out to unreached people groups. These millions who live in gross spiritual darkness have never heard the gospel. They are extremely primitive in their thinking, are idolatrous in nature, are morally anarchistic, speak in a corrupt language, have rings through their ears and noses, kill their own offspring, believe they are related to monkeys, and abide at your local university. In this "enemy territory," you are likely to encounter angry listeners controlled by worldly influences.

Could you preach at a university? Does the thought scare you? Don't let it, because universities are not filled with intelligent people who are going to run rings around you and make you look like a fool. Universities rather are filled with lost and gullible people who have been brainwashed by this blind, secular world. Always keep in mind that if you address the carnal mind with apologetics, now and then you will confront a brainiac. But all you need to do to bring in a level playing field is address the conscience with the Law.

I would also like you to keep in mind that open-air preaching is a thankless task this side of Heaven. Even more than that, it elicits the world's frown. It is a ministry of sowing in tears, of not seeing "results" at the altar, no applause, and no honorarium. When I preached in New Zealand almost daily for twelve years, I saw little fruit. It was only after I left the country to live in the United States that I started to see what God was doing. Here is one such encouraging email I received:

> I met Ray in Christchurch, New Zealand, when he was preaching in Cathedral Square. He did battle with the Official Christchurch Wizard, The Bible Lady, a guy dressed up as Sherlock Holmes, a short Chinese guy in a mini kilt and an elderly man in a raincoat who had a crowd of seagulls sitting on him. It was very colorful and quite a unique time. I was probably only 18 at that stage and my journey with God was many years away in the future. Ray was talking one day about salvation and I laughed when others laughed. Yet something Ray said then caused me to consid-

er his words. Well, nearly thirty years later (last year) I took heed of those words on the floor of an auditorium in Bulawayo, Zimbabwe (I was born again). —B. Samson, Auckland, New Zealand

You never know who is listening as you preach, or how God will use the seeds that you sow. So don't get discouraged—keep faithfully preaching, and in His timing, God will bring the increase.

"To be a soul winner is the happiest thing in this world. And with every soul you bring to Jesus Christ, you seem to get a new heaven here upon earth." —CHARLES SPURGEON

CONCLUSION

Winston Churchill failed sixth grade. He was subsequently defeated in every election for public office until he became Prime Minister at the age of sixty-two. He later wrote,

> Never give in, never give in, never, never, never, never—in nothing, great or small, large or petty—never give in except to convictions of honor and good sense. Never, never, never, never give up.

Churchill's work was temporal. Yours is eternal. He never gave up in his battle against the evil of his day. How much more should you never give up in your battle against the enemy to reach the lost! Be steadfast. Immovable. Your labor in the gospel is never, never, ever in vain.

SPURGEON'S WISDOM

Give me one hundred preachers who fear nothing but sin and desire nothing but God, and I care not whether they be clergymen or laymen, they alone will shake the gates of Hell and set up the kingdom of Heaven upon Earth.

—JOHN WESLEY

The following lengthy but wonderful quote is from a sermon by Charles Spurgeon on street preaching. Spurgeon, my favorite preacher, is known as the Prince of Preachers for good reason. One of the world's greatest open-air preachers, it's said that he could speak to a crowd of over twenty thousand people and make himself heard—without amplification. May his words of wisdom inspire you as they have me.

I am persuaded that the more of open-air preaching there is in London the better. If it should become a nuisance to some it will be a blessing to others, if properly conducted.

If it be the gospel which is spoken, and if the spirit of the preacher be one of love and truth, the results cannot be doubted: the bread cast upon the waters must be found after many days.

At the same time it must be the gospel, and be preached in a manner worth the hearing, for mere noise-making is an evil rather than a benefit. I know a family almost driven out of their senses by the hideous shouting of monotonous exhortations, and the howling of "Safe in the arms of Jesus" near their door every Sabbath afternoon by the year together. They are zealous Christians, and would willingly help their tormentors if they saw the slightest probability of usefulness from the violent bawling; but as they seldom see a hearer, and do not think that what is spoken would do any good, even if it were heard, complain that they are compelled to lose their few hours of Sabbath quiet because two good men think it their duty to perform a noisy but perfectly useless service.

I once saw a man preaching with no hearer but a dog, who sat upon his tail and looked up very reverently while his master orated. There were no people at the windows nor passing by, but the brother and his dog were at their post whether the people would hear or whether they would forbear. Once also I passed an earnest declaimer, whose hat was on the ground before him, filled with papers, and there was not even a dog for an audience, nor anyone within hearing, yet did he "waste his sweetness on the desert air." I hope it relieved his own mind. Really, it must be viewed as an essential part of a sermon that somebody should hear it: it cannot be a great benefit to the world to have sermons preached in a vacuum.

As to style in preaching out of doors, it should certainly be very different from much of that which prevails within, and perhaps if a speaker were to acquire a style fully adapted to a street audience he would be wise to bring it indoors with him. A great deal of sermonizing may be defined as saying nothing at extreme length; but out of doors verbosity is not admired, you must say something and have done with it, and go on and say something more, or your hearers will let you know. "Now then," cries a street critic, "let us have it, old fellow." Or else the observation is made, "What are you driving at? You'd better go home and learn your lesson." "Cut it short, old boy," is a very common admonition, and I wish the presenters of this advice gratis could let it be heard inside Bethel and Zoar and some other places sacred to long-winded orations. Where these outspoken criticisms are not employed, the hearers rebuke prosiness by quietly walking away. Very unpleasant this, to find your congregation dispersing, but a very plain intimation that your ideas are also much dispersed.

In the street, a man must keep himself alive, and use many illustrations and anecdotes, and sprinkle a quaint remark here and there. To dwell long on a point will never do. Reasoning must be brief, clear, and soon done with. The discourse must not be labored or involved, neither must the second head depend upon the first, for the audience is a changing one, and each point must be complete in itself. The chain of thought must be taken to pieces, and each link melted down and turned into bullets: you will need not so ranch Saladin's sabre to cut through a muslin handkerchief as Coeur de Lion's battle-ax to break a bar of iron. Come to the point at once, and come there with all your might.

Short sentences of words and short passages of thought are needed for out of doors. Long paragraphs and long arguments had better be reserved for other occasions. In quiet country crowds there is much force in an eloquent silence, now and then interjected; it gives people time to breathe, and also to reflect. A solemn pause prepares for that which is coming and has a great power over an audience. Do not, however, attempt this in a London street; there you must go ahead, or someone else may run off with your congregation. In a regular field sermon, pauses are very effective and are useful in several ways both to speaker and listeners, but to a passing company who are not inclined for anything like worship, quick, short, sharp address is most adapted.

In the streets a man must from beginning to end be intense, and for that very reason he must be condensed and concentrated in his thought and utterance. It would never do to begin by saying, "My text, dear friends, is a passage from the inspired word containing doctrines of the utmost importance, and bringing before us in the clearest manner the most valuable practical instruction. I invite your careful attention and the exercise of your most candid judgment while we consider it under various aspects and place it in different lights, in order that we may be able to perceive its position in the analogy of the faith. In its exegesis we shall find an arena for the cultured intellect and the refined sensibilities. As the purling brook meanders among the meads and fertilizes the pastures, so a stream of sacred truth flows through the remarkable words which now lie before us. It will be well for us to divert the crystal current to the reservoir of our meditation, that we may quaff the cup of wisdom with the lips of satisfaction." If you go out to the obelisk in Blackfriars Road, and talk in that fashion, you will be saluted with, "Go on, old buffer," or, "Ain't he fine! MY EYE!" A very vulgar youth will cry, "What a mouth for a rarer!" and another will shout in a tone of mock solemnity, "AMEN!"

If you give them chaff they will cheerfully return it into your own bosom. Good measure, pressed down and running over will they mete out to you. Shams and shows will have no mercy from a street gathering; but have something to say, look them in the face, say what you mean, put it plainly, boldly, earnestly, courteously, and they will hear you. Never speak against time or for the sake of hearing your own voice, or you will obtain some information about your personal appearance or manner of oratory which will probably be more true than pleasing. "Crikey," says one, "wouldn't he do for an undertaker! He'd make 'em weep": this was a compliment paid to a melancholy brother whose tone is peculiarly funereal.

"There, old fellow," said a critic on another occasion, "you go and wet your whistle. You must feel awfully dry after jawing away at that rate about nothing at all." This also was specially appropriate to a very heavy brother of whom we had afore-time remarked that he would make a good martyr, for there was no fear of his burning well, he was so dry. It is sad, very sad, that such rude remarks should be made, but there is a wicked vein in some of us, which makes us take note that the vulgar observations are often very true and "hold as 'twere the mirror up to nature." As a caricature often gives you a more vivid idea of a man than a photograph would afford you, so do these rough mob critics hit off an orator to the life by their exaggerated censures.

The very best speaker must be prepared to take his share of street wit, and to return it if need be; but primness, demureness, formality, sanctimonious long-windedness, and the affectation of superiority actually invite offensive pleasantries, and to a considerable extent deserve them. Chadband or Stiggins in rusty black, with plastered hair and huge choker, is as natural an object of derision as Mr. Guido Fawkes himself. A very great man in his own esteem will pro-yoke immediate opposition, and the affectation of supernatural saintliness will have the same effect. The less you are like a parson the more likely you are to be heard; and if you are known to be a minister, the more you show yourself to be a man the better. "What do you get for that, governor?" is sure to be asked, if you appear to be a cleric, and it will be well to tell them at once that this is extra, that you are doing overtime, and that there is to be no collection. "You'd do more good if you gave us some bread or a drop of beer, instead of those tracts," is constantly remarked, but a manly manner, and the outspoken declaration that you seek no wages but their good, will silence that stale objection.

The action of the street preacher should be of the very best. It should be purely natural and unconstrained. No speaker should stand up in the street in a grotesque manner, or he will weaken himself and invite attack. The street preacher should not imitate his own minister, or the crowd will spy out the imitation very speedily, if the brother is anywhere near home. Neither should he strike an attitude as little boys do who say, "My name is Norval." The stiff straight posture with the regular up and down motion of arm and hand is too commonly adopted, but it is not worthy of imitation: and I would even more condemn the wild raving maniac posture which some are so fond of, which seems to be a cross between Whitefield with both his arms in the air, and Saint George with both his feet violently end-aged in trampling on the dragon. Some good men are grotesque by nature, and others take great pains to make themselves so. Clumsy, heavy, jerky, cranky legs and arms appear to be liberally dispensed. Many speakers don't know what upon earth to do with these limbs, and so they stick them out, or make them revolve in the queerest manner. The wicked Londoners say, "What a cure!" I only wish I knew of a cure for the evil. All mannerisms should be avoided.

Just now I observe that nothing can be done without a very large Bagster's Bible with a limp cover. There seems to be some special charm about the large size, though it almost needs a little perambulator in which to push it about. With such a Bible, full of ribbons, select a standing in Seven Dials, after the pattern of a divine so graphically described by Mr. McCree. Take off your hat, put your Bible in it, and place it on the ground. Let the kind friend who approaches you on the right hold your umbrella. See how eager the dear man is to do so! Is it not pleasing? He assures you he is never so happy as when he is helping good men to preach to the poor sinners in these wicked places. Now close your eyes in prayer. When your devotions are over, somebody will have profited by the occasion. Where is your affectionate friend who held your umbrella and your hymn-book? Where is that well-brushed hat and that orthodox Bagster? Where? Oh where? Echo answers, "Where?"

The catastrophe which I have thus described suggests that a brother had better attend you in your earlier ministries, that one may watch while the other prays. If a number of friends will go with you and make a ring around you it will be a great acquisition; and if these can sing it will be still further helpful. The friendly company will attract others, will help to secure order, and will do good service by sounding forth sermons in song.

It will be very desirable to speak so as to be heard, but there is no use in incessant bawling. The best street preaching is not that which is done at the top of your voice, for it must be impossible to lay the proper emphasis upon telling passages when all along you are shouting with all your might. When there are no hearers near you, and yet people stand over the other side of the road and listen, would it not be as well to cross over and so save a little of the strength which is now wasted? A quiet, penetrating, conversational style would seem to be the most telling. Men do not bawl and holloa when they are pleading in deepest earnestness; they have generally at such times less wind and a little more rain; less rant and a few more tears. On, on with one monstrous shout and you will weary everybody and wear yourself out. Be wise now, therefore, O ye who would succeed in declaring your Master's message among the multitude, and use your voices as common sense would dictate.[8]

How I love and thank God for Charles Spurgeon. He could have written such wise words only from the deep wells of his own personal experience.

ANSWERS TO COMMON ARGUMENTS

To this day field preaching is a cross to me,
but I know my commission and see no other
way of preaching the gospel to every creature.

—JOHN WESLEY

For many years I have been hounded by professing Christians who have called me all sorts of names, because they believe that water baptism is necessary for salvation, or that the Sabbath must be kept, or that it's not necessary to preach repentance. Some of these people (especially the anti-repentance people) can be particularly harsh, and sometimes their words can be discouraging. I have therefore collated some of these questions, objections, and issues that continually come up to help you see the flaws in their arguments.

IS WATER BAPTISM THE NEW BIRTH?

Whenever we publish a witnessing clip where the gospel is shared with an unsaved Catholic (someone who says that they have never been born again), there are many irate comments from other Catholics insisting that the new birth spoken of in John chapter 3 is water baptism. If it is, then the Catholic who was sprinkled as an infant is saved and all is well. If it's not speaking of water baptism, then the person is unsaved and heading for Hell. So this is a vital issue. The Scriptures tell us:

> Jesus answered, "Most assuredly, I say to you, unless one is born of water and the Spirit, he cannot enter the kingdom of God. That which is born of the flesh is flesh, and that which is born of the Spirit is spirit. Do not marvel that I said to you, 'You must be born again.' The wind blows where it wishes, and you hear the sound of it, but cannot tell where it comes from and where it goes. So is everyone who is born of the Spirit." (John 3:5–8)

These are the words that some people believe refer to water baptism:

> "…unless one is born of water and the Spirit, he cannot enter the kingdom of God. That which is born of the flesh is flesh, and that which is born of the Spirit is spirit." (verse 5)

But consider the context of this verse. We are all born into this world surrounded by water. In this passage, Jesus is saying that we must be born of water *and* the Spirit. He's not saying that they are the same thing, but two separate things. Then He further confirms that the reference to water is natural human birth, by saying, "That which is born of the flesh is flesh, and that which is born of the Spirit is spirit." Again, these two are differentiated. We are all born of the flesh, surrounded by water. That's our first (physical) birth that ushers us into this world. But Jesus said that each of us must be born again (spiritual birth). We must be born of the Spirit to enter Heaven. This comes through repentance and faith in Jesus alone for our eternal salvation.

This is confirmed in Acts 2:38:

> Then Peter said to them, "Repent, and let every one of you be baptized in the name of Jesus Christ for the remission of sins; and you shall receive the gift of the Holy Spirit."

Repentance must precede water baptism. A baby has no knowledge of sin, and therefore can't repent. In addition, Jesus said,

> "The time is fulfilled, and the kingdom of God is at hand. Repent, and believe in the gospel." (Mark 1:15)

Neither can a baby "believe" the gospel. Throughout Scripture, only repentant believers are baptized. The "baptism" of a baby has no biblical basis and it has nothing to do with the new birth Jesus spoke of in John 3.

IS WATER BAPTISM ESSENTIAL FOR SALVATION?

Some believe that water baptism is essential to be saved. However, the Scriptures tell us that the Gentiles were saved *before* they were baptized in water:

> While Peter was still speaking these words, the Holy Spirit fell upon all those who heard the word. And those of the

circumcision who believed were astonished, as many as came with Peter, because the gift of the Holy Spirit had been poured out on the Gentiles also. For they heard them speak with tongues and magnify God. (Acts 10:44–46)

Notice that Scripture says "the gift of the Holy Spirit had been poured out on the Gentiles also." They had already received the gift of salvation. They had been saved and sealed by the Holy Spirit. They weren't saved by being baptized; it was God's grace alone that saved them:

> For by grace you have been saved through faith, and that not of yourselves; it is the gift of God, not of works, lest anyone should boast. (Ephesians 2:8,9)

The thief on the cross simply repented and believed. He couldn't get baptized in water, nor did he need to, because grace was enough to save him.

It was only after the Gentiles had been saved that they were then baptized in water. After acknowledging that they had already received salvation, Peter said,

> "Can anyone forbid water, that these should not be baptized who have received the Holy Spirit just as we have?" (Acts 10:47)

If water baptism were essential for salvation, the apostle Paul would have clearly said so, and would have no doubt made sure he baptized people to save them. But he didn't. He instead said, "For Christ sent me not to baptize, but to preach the gospel…" (1 Corinthians 1:17). That's because it is the *gospel* that is the power of God to salvation for everyone who believes (Romans 1:16).

ANSWERS TO COMMON ARGUMENTS

To maintain that baptism is a requirement for salvation is to add to the grace of God. It is to preach that grace isn't enough, and that flies directly in the face of Scripture.

WHEN SHOULD WE GIVE UP ON THE LOST?

I often see gentle rebukes in the comments on our YouTube videos, saying, "Don't cast your pearls before swine." This is because I'm shown pleading with someone who is clearly hardhearted and proud. Shouldn't I give up on him, and stop casting my pearls before swine?

I believe that verse is one of the most misunderstood verses in the Bible. Here's why. The greatest pearl we have is the precious pearl of the gospel. The Scriptures tell us that the preaching of the cross (the pearl of the gospel) is foolishness to those who are perishing (see 1 Corinthians 1:18). Mercy makes no sense to proud sinners. They don't value it, just as a pig doesn't value a pearl.

Think of an arrogant man who has to jump 10,000 feet out of an airplane. He's too busy enjoying the flight to worry about the coming jump and the offer of a parachute. What's the greatest favor I can do for him? Wouldn't it be to hang him out of the plane by his ankles for two seconds? Such an experience would cause him to say, "Give me that parachute!" He suddenly values it, because he has seen his terrible danger.

And so when a proud sinner sees no value in the cross, we shouldn't offer him the pearl of the gospel because he won't value it. Instead, we must hang him out into eternity by his ankles. We must go back to the threatening of the Law, and preach sin, righteousness, and judgment, so that he will value the precious mercy of God in Christ.

If any human being should be categorized as "swine," it should be Saul of Tarsus. He hated the gospel. He tortured and killed Christians for their faith in Jesus. But if you read Paul's testimony (in Romans chapter 7), you will see that it was the Law that made him tremble and brought him to the Savior on the road to Damascus.

So never give up on the proudest of souls. If a sinner mocks the cross, don't give him the comfort of the gospel because he won't value it. Instead, give him the wrath of the Law. Make him tremble. Hang him over eternity. Show this precious human being his terrible danger so that he will thirst after the righteousness that's in Christ alone.

Listen to these wonderful words of the Prince of Preachers, Charles Spurgeon:

> If sinners will be damned, at least let them leap to hell over our bodies. And if they perish, let them perish with our arms about their knees, imploring them to stay. If hell must be filled, at least let it be filled in the teeth of our exertions, and let not one go there unwarned and unprayed for.

MUST WE KEEP THE SABBATH TO BE SAVED?

Here are questions I ask those who hound me about keeping the Sabbath:

- Do you go into Jewish synagogues on the Sabbath and reason with Jews, as the apostle Paul and the disciples did?

- Do you rest on the Sabbath as you are commanded to (Exodus 20:8–11), or do you go to your church instead?

- Can you give me one New Testament verse telling Christians to keep the Jewish Sabbath? If you can, I will gladly keep it and encourage others to keep it. But there's not one.

Meanwhile, I will fellowship on the *first* day of the week, as did the disciples (see Acts 20:7). Keeping the same day the disciples kept has nothing to do with the Roman Catholic church, as some claim.

When Jesus quoted the Commandments in Mark 10:18,19, He omitted reference to the Sabbath (He made no mention of the Fourth). Neither did the apostle Paul refer to the Sabbath when he used the Law lawfully in Romans 2:21–24. I follow the examples of Jesus and Paul when reasoning with the lost.

I suggest we both obey Scripture, and instead of striving about the Law, we put our time and energy into reaching the unsaved:

But avoid foolish disputes, genealogies, contentions, and strivings about the law; for they are unprofitable and useless. (Titus 3:9)

SHOULD WE USE THE JEWISH NAME OF JESUS?

This is what I say to those who don't use the name "Jesus" but instead refer to Him as "Yeshua":

When you say the Hebrew name "Yeshua," I presume you are talking about Jesus. Here's something you may like to consider. It makes sense to use the English language when we are speaking of Jesus to English-speaking people. This is because unbelievers (those we're trying to reach) will have no idea Who we're talking about if we refer to Him in a foreign language they neither speak nor understand. We may as well be saying, "Put your faith in Ἰησοῦς Χριστός." Many to whom I have mentioned this respond by despising the name of Jesus and refusing to use it because they say that it's not His name. I trust that you're not in that category.

IS HELL MENTIONED IN THE OLD TESTAMENT?

People try to get rid of the notion of Hell by saying that it's merely a New Testament concept, and that it has no credibility because it's not mentioned in the Old Testament. Here are a few verses from the Old Testament confirming the reality of Hell.

"For a fire is kindled in My anger, and shall burn to the lowest hell; it shall consume the earth with her increase, and set on fire the foundations of the mountains." (Deuteronomy 32:22)

"The sorrows of hell compassed me about; the snares of death prevented me" (2 Samuel 22:6, KJV)

"It is as high as heaven; what canst thou do? deeper than hell; what canst thou know?" (Job 11:8, KJV)

"Hell is naked before him, and destruction hath no covering." (Job 26:6, KJV)

"The wicked shall be turned into hell, and all the nations that forget God." (Psalm 9:17)

"For thou wilt not leave my soul in hell; neither wilt thou suffer thine Holy One to see corruption." (Psalm 16:10, KJV)

"The sorrows of hell compassed me about: the snares of death prevented me." (Psalm 18:5, KJV)

"Let death seize them; let them go down alive into hell, for wickedness is in their dwellings and among them." (Psalm 55:15)

"For great is thy mercy toward me: and thou hast delivered my soul from the lowest hell." (Psalm 86:13, KJV)

"The sorrows of death compassed me, and the pains of hell gat hold upon me: I found trouble and sorrow." (Psalm 116:3, KJV)

"If I ascend into heaven, You are there; if I make my bed in hell, behold, You are there." (Psalm 139:8)

"Her feet go down to death, her steps lay hold of hell." (Proverbs 5:5)

"Her house is the way to hell, descending to the chambers of death." (Proverbs 7:27)

"But he does not know that the dead are there, that her guests are in the depths of hell." (Proverbs 9:18)

"Hell and Destruction are before the LORD; so how much more the hearts of the sons of men." (Proverbs 15:11)

"The way of life winds upward for the wise, that he may turn away from hell below." (Proverbs 15:24)

"You shall beat him with a rod, and deliver his soul from hell." (Proverbs 23:14)

"Hell and Destruction are never full; so the eyes of man are never satisfied." (Proverbs 27:20)

"Therefore hell hath enlarged herself, and opened her mouth without measure: and their glory, and their multitude, and their pomp, and he that rejoiceth, shall descend into it." (Isaiah 5:14, KJV)

"Hell from beneath is excited about you, to meet you at your coming; it stirs up the dead for you, all the chief ones of the earth; it has raised up from their thrones all the kings of the nations." (Isaiah 14:9)

IS HELL MENTIONED IN THE NEW TESTAMENT?

Those who don't believe in a literal hell often say that it merely means the grave. But the word "grave" doesn't fit into these verses, nor are they metaphoric:

"But I say to you that whoever is angry with his brother without a cause shall be in danger of the judgment. And whoever says to his brother, 'Raca!' shall be in danger of the council. But whoever says, 'You fool!' shall be in danger of hell fire." (Matthew 5:22)

"If your right eye causes you to sin, pluck it out and cast it from you; for it is more profitable for you that one of your members perish, than for your whole body to be cast into hell." (Matthew 5:29)

"And if your right hand causes you to sin, cut it off and cast it from you; for it is more profitable for you that one of your members perish, than for your whole body to be cast into hell." (Matthew 5:30)

"And do not fear those who kill the body but cannot kill the soul. But rather fear Him who is able to destroy both soul and body in hell." (Matthew 10:28)

"And if your eye causes you to sin, pluck it out and cast it from you. It is better for you to enter into life with one eye, rather than having two eyes, to be cast into hell fire." (Matthew 18:9)

"Woe to you, scribes and Pharisees, hypocrites! For you travel land and sea to win one proselyte, and when he is won, you make him twice as much a son of hell as yourselves." (Matthew 23:15)

"Serpents, brood of vipers! How can you escape the condemnation of hell?" (Matthew 23:33)

"If your hand causes you to sin, cut it off. It is better for you to enter into life maimed, rather than having two hands, to go to hell, into the fire that shall never be quenched." (Mark 9:43)

"And if your foot causes you to sin, cut it off. It is better for you to enter life lame, rather than having two feet, to be cast into hell, into the fire that shall never be quenched." (Mark 9:45)

"And if your eye causes you to sin, pluck it out. It is better for you to enter the kingdom of God with one eye, rather than having two eyes, to be cast into hell fire." (Mark 9:47)

"But I will show you whom you should fear: Fear Him who, after He has killed, has power to cast into hell; yes, I say to you, fear Him!" (Luke 12:5)

Are you "warning every man" as Scripture commands? Do you say with Paul, "Knowing, therefore, the terror of the Lord, we persuade men" (2 Corinthians 5:11)?

IS JESUS GOD IN HUMAN FORM?

Many sincere Christians are confused when they hear that God was manifest in human form, because they read that Jesus was the "Son" of God.

"And without controversy great is the mystery of godliness:
God was manifested in the flesh,
Justified in the Spirit,
Seen by angels,
Preached among the Gentiles,
Believed on in the world,
Received up in glory." (1 Timothy 3:16)

"In the beginning was the Word, and the Word was with God, and the Word was God. He was in the beginning with God. All things were made through Him, and without Him nothing was made that was made... And the Word became flesh and dwelt among us, and we beheld His glory, the glory as of the only begotten of the Father, full of grace and truth." (John 1:1–3,14)

"He has delivered us from the power of darkness and conveyed us into the kingdom of the Son of His love, in whom we have redemption through His blood, the forgiveness of sins. He is the image of the invisible God, the firstborn over all creation. For by Him all things were created that are in heaven and that are on earth, visible and invisible, whether thrones or dominions or principalities or powers. All things were created through Him and for Him. And He is before all things, and in Him all things consist." (Colossians 1:13–17)

"Therefore, when Christ enters into the world, He says, 'Sacrifice and offering You have not desired, but [instead] You have prepared a body for Me [to offer].'" (Hebrews 10:5, AMP)

"For unto us a Child is born, unto us a Son is given; and the government will be upon His shoulder. And His name will be called Wonderful, Counselor, Mighty God, Everlasting Father, Prince of Peace." (Isaiah 9:6)

NOTES

1. Further details of this are available in *Out of the Comfort Zone* (Bridge-Logos).

2. This series would be very helpful for you to learn how to open-air preach: <tinyurl.com/y9vo6oao>.

3. The flipchart is available on LivingWaters.com as a free download, and the Trivia Book is available in a laminated spiral-bound version.

4. For some interesting interviews on the scientific basis of evolution, see "Evolution vs. God," and for insights into why atheists choose to believe in evolution, watch "The Atheist Delusion" (both available free at LivingWaters.com/movies).

5. John Wesley, Sermon 43: "The Scripture Way of Salvation" <tinyurl.com/h7zxdgw>.

6. Charles Spurgeon, Sermon 460: "Faith and Repentance Inseparable," July 13, 1862 <tinyurl.com/y6tkg8yl>.

7. Watch "Noah and the Last Days" (NoahTheMovie.com) and other videos to see how this is done.

8. Charles Spurgeon, "Street Preaching," *The Sword and the Trowel*, November 1876 <tinyurl.com/ydgrk64a>.

RESOURCES

For assistance in getting started in open-air-preaching, see the following resources on LivingWaters.com:

Springboards for Budding Preachers: These transcripts of dozens of open-air sessions, available as a PDF, will provide helpful tips and illustrations to capture and keep your audience's attention. (Also available for Kindle on Amazon.)

Open Air Trivia Book (spiral bound) and **Open-Air Flipchart** (downloadable PDF) to use as visuals for trivia questions.

Open-Air Preaching: New York, 40 Years of Open-Air Preaching, and **The Angry Atheist** (MP4 videos) to see preaching in a variety of settings dealing with a variety of issues.

Hell's Best Kept Secret / True and False Conversion: Listen to these vital messages free at HellsBestKeptSecret.com.

God Has a Wonderful Plan for Your Life: The Myth of the Modern Message: Our most important book (over 350,000 in print).

For additional tips on evangelism and apologetics, please visit our website where you can sign up for our free weekly e-mail update. You can also gain further insights by watching the weekly TV program *Way of the Master* (WayoftheMaster.com), as well as countless videos on our LivingWaters YouTube channel, with over 270,000,000 views.

For a complete list of resources by Ray Comfort, visit **LivingWaters.com**, call 800-437-1893, or write to: Living Waters Publications, P.O. Box 1172, Bellflower, CA 90706.

THE EVIDENCE STUDY BIBLE

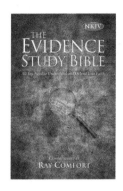

"An invaluable tool for becoming a more effective witness." —FRANKLIN GRAHAM

The Evidence Study Bible (NKJV) arms you not just with apologetic information to refute the arguments of skeptics, but with practical evangelism training on how to lead them to Christ.

- Discover answers to over 200 questions such as: Why is there suffering? How could a loving God send people to hell? What about those who never hear of Jesus?

- In addition to thousands of verse-related comments, over 130 informative articles will enable you to better comprehend and communicate the Christian faith.

- Over two dozen articles on evolution will thoroughly prepare you to refute the theory.

- Dozens of articles on other religions will help you understand and address the beliefs of Mormons, Hindus, Muslims, Jehovah's Witnesses, cults, and others.

- Hundreds of inspiring quotes from renowned Christian leaders and practical tips on defending your faith will greatly encourage and equip you.

The Evidence Study Bible provides powerful and compelling evidence that will enrich your trust in God and His Word, deepen your love for the truth, and enable you to reach those you care about with the message of eternal life.

Commended by Norman Geisler, Josh McDowell,
D. James Kennedy, Woodrow Kroll, Tim LaHaye,
Ken Ham, and many other Christian leaders

School of Biblical Evangelism

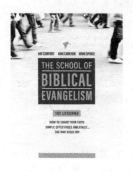

Do you want to deepen your passion for the lost, for the cross, and for God? Then look no further. Join more than 25,000 students from around the world in the School of Biblical Evangelism, to learn how to witness and defend the faith.

With 101 lessons on subjects ranging from basic Christian doctrines to knowing our enemy, from false conversions to proving the deity of Jesus, you will be well-equipped to answer questions as you witness to anyone. This study course will help you to prove the authenticity of the Bible, provide ample evidence for creation, refute the claims of evolution, understand the beliefs of those in cults and other religions, and know how to reach both friends and strangers with the gospel.

"A phenomenal course."
—Jim Culver

"Awesome… This course should be required in every theological seminary."
—Spencer S. Hanley

"As a graduate of every other evangelism course I can find, yours by far has been the best."
—Bill Lawson

"I have never seen anything as powerful as the teaching in the School of Biblical Evangelism."
—James W. Smith

Join online at **www.biblicalevangelism.com**
or, to obtain the entire course in book form,
call **800-437-1893** or visit fine bookstores everywhere